*Music's Handmaid*

# Music's Handmaid

by

## HARRIET COHEN

**FABER AND FABER LTD**

24 Russell Square

London

*First published in mcmxxxvi*
*by Faber and Faber Limited*
*24 Russell Square London W.C.1*
*Reissued in this new edition mcml*
*Printed in Great Britain by*
*Latimer Trend & Co Ltd Plymouth*

To

## ARNOLD BAX

The poetry that lies too deep for words does not lie too deep for music.

GEORGE BERNARD SHAW

# *Contents*

## PART I: THE COMPOSER

## PART II: THE PERFORMER

## PART III: THE TECHNIQUE OF THE APPROACH TO MUSIC

# *Acknowledgements*

I wish to thank Ralph Bates for his devoted help and assistance in research.

I should also like to acknowledge with thanks permission to reproduce music quotations as follows:

To the Oxford University Press for permission to use extracts from Hymn Tune Prelude by Vaughan Williams on pp. 149, 151 and 152.

To Messrs. J. and W. Chester Lt.d for quotations in my lessons on de Falla and Bax.

To Messrs. Boosey and Hawkes for permission to quote from Bartok's Mikrokosmos on pp. 155, 156 and 160.

# *Note*

It is to persuade students to enlarge their idiomatic grasp and to come into more intense possession of the inner spirit of music, that I have chosen to preface the chapters on Analysis, Interpretation and Technique, which make up the bulk of this book, with what in effect is an attempt to express my personal approach to modern music, by way of the old. My reasons for doing so will, I hope, rapidly become evident.

# Part I: The Composer

⭐

Whosoever is harmonically composed, delights in harmony; which makes me much distrust the symmetry of those heads which declaim against all Church-Musick. For myself, not only from my obedience, but my particular Genius, I do embrace it: for even that vulgar and Tavern-Musick, which makes one man merry, another mad, strikes in me a deep fit of devotion, and a profound contemplation of the first Composer.—SIR THOMAS BROWNE.

# CHAPTER I

## *Discords and Concords*

Discords mingled with concords not onlie are tollerable, but make the des-cant more pleasing if they will be well taken—Moreover, there is no coming to a close, speciallie with a Cadence, without a discord.—THOMAS MORLEY, *A Plane and Easie Introduction to Practical Musiche*, 1597.

I have often been asked why it is that I, who have devoted so much of my time to making known the beauty of early keyboard music, choose also to include in my programmes so many modern pianoforte works. Behind this question lies the often expressed opinion that modern composers are destructive of all that loveliness which the sixteenth-and seventeenth-century music contains.

Now in order to make clear why I think that the student owes both himself and his art the duty of trying to understand contemporary music we may listen to the following imaginary dialogue between a fourteenth-century defender of tradition and one of the most considerable of innovators. Johannes de Muris, who was born in the thirteenth century and who practised well into the fourteenth century, was one of the most famous and favoured of conservative theoreticians and teachers. It would be very unfair to call him a pure reactionary, however. The person I have chosen as his opponent is

Philippe de Vitry who, born in the thirteenth century, died in
1361. Philippe could not have expressed all the ideas he puts
forward here, but it is good that his name should be remembered. When we come upon them in the cloister of a French
cathedral, perhaps, they have been debating for more than
two hours, and the crudities and incivilities of debate (and there
were many of the latter for all the decorum of scholarly custom) have been dispensed with. Both contestants are at grips
in earnest. Manuscripts of the great doctors and the learned
commentators on Aristotle lie around them, their pages rising and falling in the breeze, their brilliant and lovely illum-
inations glowing like jewels where the infiltring beam of the
sun strikes them.

JOHANNES: I assert that tradition, consolidated and brought
to orderly principles by scholars and doctors cannot be broken.
Without a knowledge of such tradition music cannot be made.
Why, sir, there are those who actually compose descant when
they know precisely nothing of the nature of consonance, and
if by good luck they stumble upon a concord such is their
ignorance that they at once proceed to a discord.

PHILIPPE: But sir—for I recognize that you refer to me—
has it not appeared to you that what you have chosen to call
'discord' is but a new consonance. It is a question both of
intelligent extension of theory and of accustoming one's
ear.

JOHANNES: But I tell you that your excessive discords dis-
may the music lover, so that when you should delight you
merely cause depression.

So far many will find themselves in agreement with
Johannes, but now listen to the second disputant's retort.

PHILIPPE: And I for my part declare that your consonance,

18

as you call it, of fourths and fifths and octaves wearies me. Why should not thirds and sixths be regarded as consonances?

JOHANNES: The principles of descant are known to you. . . .

PHILIPPE: And I declare that your music admits too little feeling.

JOHANNES: There, sir, you fall foul of the gravity of our art. I find your music full of exaggerated sentiment like the music of the people who know nothing of the theory of music. Thirds and sixths, sir! that is how the barbarian English do sing.

PHILIPPE: It is for the enrichment of our art; I declare that your art is constricted and lifeless, and that the common people have more delight in singing than we. . . .

And now Johannes makes a familiar point.

JOHANNES: And I insist that you abandon repose with your innovation of headlong and vulgar rhythm. Music that is not composed in one of the Six Rhythmical Modes. . . .

PHILIPPE: The Six Rhythmical Modes! I am bored to extinction by your eternal triple rhythms!

JOHANNES (*raising his voice*): And as I said in my letter to *The Times*, I deny that duple time has any place in art!

PHILIPPE: Yet sir, the practice of music is deciding now in favour of these innovations as you call them, all of which have been so long part of the music of popular tradition.

Whereupon Johannes stamps out, muttering 'cacophonous stuff! Modern Music indeed', and 'your innovations in notation, too!'

In this imaginary discourse I have made no points that are not part of the great *Ars Nova* debate, in part disputed in Johannes de Muris's *Speculum musice* which is preserved in a manuscript of about 1323. Many of the complaints put into his mouth have been taken from that work. For Philippe de Vitry's views one must go to his *Ars Nova* written about the same time, though I have also drawn upon other sources.

Now my intention will not be grasped until it is realized that to many music lovers Johannes was right. True, there were many composers such as Guillaume de Machault (1300–77) who availed themselves of Philippe's 'licences', while a wave of discontent with old rules, and of searching after greater expressiveness was being felt throughout Europe. It was an unrest, an urge of the age. Philippe de Vitry's music unfortunately has all disappeared, but that of de Machault has survived.

And despite excesses, it really is true that *Ars Nova* immediately accomplished something worth while, for Guillaume's Mass in Four Parts is the second earliest contrapuntal mass known to us. His Rondeaux and Ballades too are polyphonic, so that he was really extending the use as well as enriching the technique of counterpoint. And whereas few but antiquaries could find continuous delight in music written before Johannes de Muris (in Adam de la Hali's *Hareu li maus d'amer ochist* parallel fourths are the principal harmonic device), de Machault's Chansons Balladées possess for us no little beauty. It is well to remember, however, that Guillaume was quite capable of writing five parallel sevenths which might have served the Stravinsky of the Sacre with a model.

I have not written this in order to prove that conservative critics are necessarily wrong, or that innovation is an unmixed blessing, but in order to establish exactly what it is musical innovators do and why they do it. From the results I think we may obtain some kind of principles which may serve as criteria in testing the validity of twentieth-century innovations.

The work of the *Ars Nova* musicians discloses two things:

(1) They were extending the technique of music, by the introduction of new consonances and by new use of discords, thus developing and indeed inaugurating counterpoint. They were developing technique also by introducing new rhythms.

(2) They were doing this under the influence of spiritual necessities, in order to achieve greater expressiveness. That was, in general, in response to the spirit of the age.

Is it too much to say that but for the achievements of Ars Novists the music of that age would have languished, perhaps have been frustrated?

Now most innovations lead to excesses and we have to remember that such as Johannes de Muris were often really protesting against those excesses, rather than the fact of *some* change. Let us see what happened.

There is in the British Museum a delightful little book printed in 1649, written by John IV of Portugal. It is called *A Defense of Modern Music* and in it the Portuguese king answers the complaints of a certain Bishop Cyrilo Franco, who in 1549 wrote a letter to one Ugolino Gualteruzio in very robustly critical terms. Now it is to be noted that the bishop was writing long after the *Ars Nova* theories had produced their results and before the next considerable innovation of vertical harmony in music had been accomplished. His opponent, John IV, however, replies to him from the vantage point of that innovatory age.

The bishop is, I fear, a rather crochety gentleman, for all his being a ghost, and finds fault with everything.

THE BISHOP: And it has come to this pass that one hears

people say: 'They sang a pretty mass to-day in the chapel.' Ask them what mass it was and they will reply: 'The Armed Man' or 'Hercules, Duke of Ferrara'. Now what the devil has music to do with an armed man or with the Duke of Ferrara, may I ask?

(The vigorous expression is the bishop's, not mine.)

JOHN IV: Oh, but reverend father, one must have names, and why not take the names of the themes the masses are composed upon?

THE BISHOP: Well, I want music to be expressive, to move the spirit, and I find that this modern stuff doesn't accomplish half as much as the old, nor is it so well adapted to the letter. There's nothing good in it except perhaps the pavane and the galliard.

JOHN IV: Reverend father! Surely modern music is even more moving than the old. Think of that passage in Lorenzo Rebello's psalm *Qui habitat* at the words *non timebis a timore nocturno*. [And he gives a whole list of such 'effects' as we nowadays call them.] And indeed the music of Lucas Marencio, Claudio Monteverde and the Principe de Venosa has huge power to move the spirit. If it doesn't, then neither the music nor the composer is at fault!

THE BISHOP (*glaring at the insinuation*): But I want my sacred music to be different from my profane, and I want my Kyrie eleison to be different from my Sanctus. And besides, modern musicians put all their endeavours into so tying up their music in fugues that when one sings Sanctus another is singing Sabaoth and another Gloria tua, so that what with howling, bellowings and bawlings they more resemble cats in January than flowers in May!

JOHN IV: As for that tying up in fugues I grant you things

22

went too far, as also in the matter of making ecclesiastical music different from profane. Yet we have now the masses of Palestrina which admirably do this.

It is clear that the king is claiming Palestrina as part of the modern movement. He means, of course, that he utilizes the contrapuntal skill elaborated in the years following the *Ars Nova* debate. Actually, I think, for all the transcendental loveliness of the music, Palestrina was something of a reactionary and it is to Vittoria I should direct students for an example of a great contrapuntalist whose music strives to achieve the maximum permissible of expressiveness. The intensity of feeling, the mystical fervour and the dramatic power, sometimes excessive, of Vittoria, are far too little appreciated in this country.

But it is noteworthy that John IV, who has approved of Monteverde and the Prince of Venosa should advance the name of Palestrina, for it shows a recognition of the idea of *fitness for purpose*.

Now it is interesting to note all that has happened. First there is a movement towards greater expressiveness, employing an advanced technique, then the delight and extravagance in the use of that technique defeats one of its original purposes, the securing of expressiveness. Moreover, the protest against uniformity and regimentation has led to licence. I say 'for purpose' because a technique that creates intelligible music is its own justification.

Then, the desire for expressiveness takes the form of not only rhythmical adjustment of the music to the words in choral music, but of what might be called incidentalism or pictorialism. This is one of the most characteristic practices of our own great Elizabethan school of madrigalists and itself led to harmonic innovations, some of which were contested and even thought a little audacious by the composers themselves. William Byrd in The Epistle to the Reader contained in his *Psalmes, Sonets and Songs* of 1588 says:

'In the expressing of these songs, either by Voyces or Instruments, if there be any jarre or dissonance, blame not the Printer who (I doe assure thee) . . . doth heere deliver to thee a perfect and true Coppie.'

Byrd, by the way, is referring to the simultaneous use of major and minor thirds. That such things are even now occasionally regarded as crudities one may see from the fact that a twentieth-century scholar can say 'occasionally the simultaneous occurrence of the major and minor third gives an effect that is by no means cacophonous even to modern ears'. And harmonic liberties so achieved were not invariably attached to the props of interpretative necessity. They took status of their own and, had there not occurred a tragical severance of the English tradition of music, the history of contrapuntal theory might have been very different.

It is in this glorious music that we find the finest expression of the rhythmic principles brought into music by preceding innovatory epochs. In proof of the contention that I shall later develop that the intellectual approach to modern music exactly matches in type of effort that which one needs for approaching *any* music, especially if it be ever so little outside of the general tradition, I advance these observations. It is in his remarks about the madrigalists that Burney, on the whole a sensible man, comments on their 'broken phrases and false accents of the melody, in which there is so total a want of rhythm as renders the time extremely difficult to keep with accuracy and firmness'. He thought, moreover, that Farmer, who had claimed to have linked the words with his music with especial care 'exhibited more false accent in his songs than did his contemporaries'. Of course! Burney's error comes through not appreciating the rhythmic idiom of the music of that period. And nowadays, when the distinction between barred and unbarred music is made upon all hands, how often do we hear Elizabethan music played with correct and sensitive placing of the accent?

From the standpoint of one hardened by the material discipline of nineteenth-century music it is indeed a difficult thing to think in terms of the sixteenth-century idiom. Is it not significant that the revival of interest in early music is more or less coincident in time with a period of experimentation in technique and aesthetics? That modern changes in outlook can definitely assist us in this way is argued by this passage from a book by Mr. Cecil Gray and the late Philip Heseltine on that extraordinary early seventeenth-century composer, Gesualdo Prince of Venosa. Of the Prince's *Moro lasso al mio duolo* they say: 'Things of this kind most certainly have seemed crude and tentative, fantastic almost to the point of insanity, to the historians of the eighteenth and nineteenth centuries. . . . In the light of the musical developments of the last five and twenty years, however, we see them not as stammering and experimental utterances in a new idiom, but as miracles of perfected craft and expression.' And whereas Burney regards the Prince of Venosa's music as full of barbarities and unprincipled modulation and depravity of style, Messrs. Gray and Heseltine consider it to be a reaching out beyond tonality in the manner of some modern composers who juxtapose chords theoretically related. That may be, of course, because tonality as we understand it was not yet rigidly defined or clearly understood in Gesualdo's day. Nowadays we see that Gesualdo was a very definite individualist, though he gained the admiration of most lovers of music, especially the amateurs of his day.

To the conservatives of his day, however, Gesualdo seemed to be no more than another expression of the movement centred round Claudio Monteverde. From the Monteverdean controversy at least one more important consideration can be derived. Monteverde's adversary shall be Canon Artusi, a learned and conservative theoretician who in the year 1600 published a delightful book of controversial dialogues called *L'Artusi overo della imperfetione della Musica moderna* to which Monteverde replied in the preface to his Fifth Book of Madrigals.

ARTUSI: I assert that tradition consolidated and brought to orderly principles by scholars and doctors cannot be broken without loss. Why, sir, there are those who actually compose madrigals without regard to the rules of counterpoint! I say that the licentious innovations such people make will end by destroying the art of counterpoint altogether, and there are, sir, already composers who know nothing of counterpoint.

MONTEVERDE: Venerable father, as to your last remark I would point out that I compose my ecclesiastical music with the stoutest regard for the rules of counterpoint. In fact, sir, whereas Master Palestrina sets his face against certain liberties such as of the Venice school, I deliberately set my face against many others. Is not my contrapuntal music as severe, almost as archaic in style, if you like, as that of Joaquin des Près; and there is in it no theatricality, is there?

ARTUSI: That may be as you say, yet Master Palestrina has written madrigals in a pure contrapuntal style. What you in your ignorance are doing will, I repeat, destroy counterpoint.

MONTEVERDE: I reply that I am not composing in ignorance, that I am writing as I write deliberately, and confessedly —not as those who write pamphlets against me under false names. [Artusi, having done this, looks a little sheepish.] I say, sir, that there exists *another system* of harmony besides that which you expound. Master Palestrina's madrigals are too smooth, it is beyond the power of counterpoint to be dramatic and expressive enough for that kind of writing.

ARTUSI: You seek to delight sense rather than reason.

MONTEVERDE: Has not sense, as you call it, its reason too? The old composers of madrigals thought too much of structure and not enough to translate into music the emotions suggested by poetry. For the theatre and the *salon* the new system, for the Church, the old. And the new system, sir, has in truth been a long time in vogue. Does it not really begin to appear with the first madrigals that were written?

In this dialogue which accurately represents the 'modern music' debate of that period we see again the concept of *fitness for purpose*. Moreover, Artusi is definitely correct within his limits. Monteverde's innovations did end by doing as the Canon declared they would. He is wrong in not perceiving that a new idiom was emerging which might possess value. Possibly not even Monteverde realized that tonality in its eighteenth-and nineteenth-century implication was also being born.

# CHAPTER II

# Idioms and Innovations

The object of music is to conjure God, to put the Devil to flight, to heal the sick and to provoke love.—JOHANNES DE TINCTORIS. *Maestro di capillo* at Court of Ferdinand of Aragon, King of Naples from 1475 to 1487.

Cantilena charms the hearers and incites them to the love of virtue. But music has a power such that if it employs modes more agreeable than is necessary, it leads spirits into weakness. If it employs austere and solemn movements it is a stimulant to courage and the spiritual life.—SIMON TUNSTEDE. Fourteenth-century theoretician.

The three 'Modern Music' debates which we have just investigated cannot fail to make our truth clear, that the controversy about innovation is a permanent feature of our art. And about that controversy perhaps the most striking thing is that its charges and counter-charges are practically always the same, often, indeed, its very terms are identical. It is amusing, too, to notice that Johannes de Muris, Bishop Cyrilo Franco and Canon Artusi might almost be discussing twentieth-century music.

But it was to discover critical principles useful in our approach to modern music that we began this exercise, and that without more delay we must attempt to do. Let us set out our observations in orderly fashion.

## Motivation of change

Profitable innovations have always had as motive profound spiritual needs, and these needs—that is to say, the expression of feeling—are of the kind that lie at the very root and origin of music. They are gradual in emergence, and widespread and social in character, rather than individual. By even such a broadly stated criterion as this, some musical innovations are clearly frivolous. No musician should have been deceived by the now forgotten manifestos of the twenties. It is not liberative of creative impulse, for instance, to know that 'Dada is a virgin microbe'.

The extent to which an age may desire its emotional flow to be expressive will vary, of course, and it may often be that a period of excess will cause a revulsion against feeling, for an overload of sentiment is quite the worst of ancestral builders. Yet such frosty climes as were visited by Stravinsky in the Wind Instrument period surely lie outside the province of the art. Indeed, I think that Stravinsky has denied himself just that very impulse which was most fertile in his art. He is really a pre-Russian, a Scythian, and a Scythian struggling against the Slav. That conflict of two immense urges vitalized him, and his music loses interest from the moment the theorizing Western takes control. Deeply as one may desire, not a return but an advance to classicisms of form and reticence, one distrusts *personal* conversions, as much as one distrusts the revulsion as a directive force. Not that way have the great periods been initiated. The function of the great individual is really to take up and transform what has been communally produced. The Prince of Venosa is but one who has created so.

New life and an invigorating enrichment of feeling were given to fourteenth-century music when such innovators as Philippe de Vitry and Guillaume de Machault began to make use of the tradition and technique of popular music. In the latter years of the nineteenth century exactly the same thing was done for Spanish music by musical scholars, the chief of whom was Felipe Pedrell. Pedrell claimed that the only way to reinvigorate the music of Spain was to go back to the popular music of folk song and dance, still uncontaminated by alien influences and urban corruptions, and only in this way, he urged, could Spanish musical minds be placed in contact with the true national feeling, or regain the idiom natural to racial temperament. Felipe Pedrell although his opera *Los Pireneos* contains much beautiful music, is to be regarded rather more as a preacher and precursor than as one who himself achieved his regrafting of contemporary Spanish music on to its ancient and still healthy stock. (Indeed, Eric Blom writes that 'beyond the adoption of a national Spanish musical idiom he brought no new element into dramatic music'.) Such men as Albeniz, Granados and Turina and above all Manuel de Falla, however, have really succeeded in doing this. Even when, as in the case of de Falla, some of this fine music is not textually based upon popular melodies, or even upon similar types of theme, those who understand the Spanish temperament will always recognize the national idiom (a very different thing from the mere scale and colouring which pseudo-hispanists employ to give 'Spanish' effects).

In the case of the piece chosen for a lesson in a later chapter all this is particularly true. Not only are the dances of *The Three-Cornered Hat* often highly stylized uses of the great Andalusian dance rhythms, but the story of the ballet itself is a folk tale of the Andalusian sierras. Don Pedro Alarcón, whose famous version of it in *El Corregidor* (incidentally one of the finest long, short-stories ever written), was the first to make the story widely known, indeed claimed no more for his work than that it was the best version of a story common among shepherds and mountain dwellers in his home region. It was this splendid folk tale, shapely and vivid as it is and full of wit and understanding also, that provided Martinez Sierra with the subject of the ballet composed by Falla for the late M. Diaghileff.

It is at this point that I should like to draw attention to the real nature of idiom. One may profitably compare it with linguistic idiom. Such expressions as 'black as a wolf's throat' as a description of a very dark night or 'to put oneself into a shirt eleven yards long' as meaning to meddle with other people's business, are often described as idioms of the French and Spanish languages respectively. They would be better called idiosyncrasies. An exhaustive list of such expressions will tell one less about the real nature of the Latin group of languages than an understanding of the significance of reflexive verbs, or say, the difference between 'ser' and 'estar' in Spanish. The difference in ancient Greek (or modern Russian, so I am told) between the two forms of verb, one for definite limited actions and the other for continuous states of doing or being is also truly idiomatic. It expresses a fundamental way of thinking which the above expressions do not.

Similarly with music; quite casual examination of a composer's music will disclose certain frequently returning modes or devices which are often called idioms. Such a thing as the facile type of left-hand figures to be found in profusion in Mozart's pianoforte sonatas is an example of this, yet what has

31

this figuration to do with the essential thought of Mozart? The fastidious and subtle rhythmic flow, the contrast and complement of rhythms, the perfect balance that they achieve so that the rhythmic vitality seems to be ever welling up into the music; this is a real Mozartian musical idiom, expressing in perfect proportion the wit, the grace, the irony and the sentiment of his mental idiom. And in general I think that an appreciation of a composer's line and rhythmic impulses is much more vital to an understanding of him than a study of his harmony.

To a large extent the composer who is in perfect control of his personal idiom is often unaware of some characteristic feature of his work. Sibelius once told me that he did not notice that his sixth Symphony was a modal work, while Arnold Bax has often commented to me upon the fact that he had written four symphonies before he discovered that they possessed one characteristic form.

The technique which upon the 'material' side of the art corresponds to the spiritual impulses will usually be found to be rooted in the past. Proof of this is unwittingly disclosed by such revolutionaries as Marinetti who wished to blow all Jericho flat with a muted trumpet. How often they defend their positions by pointing out that Bach or Mozart had done it before. The same thing is true of pictorial art. Cubism can be found in some of Albrecht Dürer's work we are told, or in some twelfth-century Vatican manuscript, which none but a few scholars have seen, Mount Sinai is drawn as a cube. Or it is said that Van Gogh had good authority for his technique of laying lines of colour side by side, because it has been discovered that the shadows of the nose in a certain portrait by Ghirlandaio are composed of thin lines of red and green. The mode of argument is reasonable, though it not infrequently happens that a feature which a great artist admits to be a defect or incapacity in his work will be taken as an essential by revolutionary enthusiasts. The bare patches of canvas in Cézanne provide an illustration.

But returning to music, the reason why one distrusts the more violent innovations is that on the *technical* side they often do not spring out of *musical* necessities, but proceed from abstract aesthetics or scientific reasoning. It is important to understand this dual nature of idiomatic advance. Spiritual needs are the urge to innovation, and these innovations can only be fruitful when they exert their impulse through the channels of emotion. So long as polyphony was capable of technical development it could accept the strain of new impulses (and these are usually only *deepenings* or extensions of impulse); or from the other point of view, and both are valid, the improvements in contrapuntal technique permitted the fuller expression of pre-existent feeling. There is nothing mystical about this stipulation of emotional or spiritual necessity. If a particular problem is presented to a large number of composers at the same period, then obviously it stands much more chance of solution, and when solved will receive great enrichment.

To make the discussion concrete one may take the case of Schönberg. It is true that chromaticism had begun to destroy tonality and that the generally accepted need of tonality was something which seemed to limit chromaticism. Thus the division of the octave into twelve semitones of equal harmonic importance and the consequent deliberate destruction of tonality represent a process of necessity which at least had some pressure behind it. It is folly to say that great music cannot be written with such a technique, but that does not compel us to acclaim Schönberg as a great composer—powerful though his influence on contemporary music may be. I must not be misunderstood here; our art needs technical pioneers, and delight in technical mastery undoubtedly *has* advanced music; but I distrust the emotional integrity of experimentation that Schönberg indulged in when still young. It does not seem a sincere effort to write first a succession of common inversions and then by deliberate mechanical distortion of notes in that sequence to produce new harmonic results. Such exercises seem to me to disclose an absolutely non-musical kind of interest, which if persevered in could only lead to barren intellectualism. This *extra*-musical interest and quality of Schönberg seems evident from the inner content of his art. In such works as the Five Orchestral Pieces, the heroic steed of Wagnerism cavorting amidst a Covent Garden conflagration has been grotesquely diminished to a gaunt and fleshless sea-horse poking furtively among atonal weeds.

If what I have said about Schönberg appears to be unduly stringent, I do not wish to detract from his very definite achievements. Sometimes I fancifully wish that he had invented a new art, somewhere between music and mathematics, in which he would have been supreme. Like the conventional north, Schönberg's orientation is surely a little to the east of the true magnetic pole of music.

As to what were the prime emotional impulses in this atonal experimentation it is not for me to guess. It seems evident, however, that such a technique must open up new areas of feeling or extend old ones enormously. It must do this to be justified, and I think that Alban Berg has shown us in what direction it will operate. Such music seems to me to be the musical equivalent of very subtle and highly introspective analysis of psychological states. It is perhaps inevitable that at our present stage of understanding of and response to atonal music, such analyses must seem peculiarly personal. That may explain the intense self-consciousness which I feel to be the chief characteristic of Berg's music. There may be a future for such music if as in the case of Luigi Dallapiccola it receives its impulse from a more universal mood.

Atonality, however, is undoubtedly an idiom (though in idea not quite so new as is sometimes supposed), and we must not close our ears to music in that idiom. Certain non-musical speculations should incline us towards a kind of neutral benevolence at least. Literature has been more and more impelled to concern itself with introspective states. This may indeed be a regrettable tendency, but none can deny that it exists. The large dramatic clashes of Man with Fate of the Greek Drama, superseded by the struggles of Man with Institution, then of man and man in the drama of acquisitive passions, has given way to the struggle of man with himself. Busoni's *Faust* might stand as the supreme example of this movement. Alban Berg's *Wozzeck* and *Lulu* are others. Undoubtedly the partial success of scientific modes of inquiry into psychology has made man self-conscious in a quite peculiar way. The drama of life has become cerebral and nervous and inhibited, rather than active, passionate and explosive. Yet the values of drama have remained, weakened no doubt and hindered in expression by difficulties of form, for the older forms and idioms of art are clearly unsuited to this highly pitched material. Nevertheless, they do remain, and just as the emergence of a more personal kind of drama in the time of Monteverde brought with it the vertical harmony with its disintegration of texture, the current trend is in the direction of yet subtler and for the time being equally disintegrating techniques. In the concert room Alban Berg may not be quite convincing—there is less doubt about his success in the theatre.

In passing, it is curious to note that the period which saw the beginning of the modern harmonic idiom, principally inspired by dramatic and emotional requirements, saw also more than one attempt in the direction of a kind of atonality. The chromaticism of such as Orlando di Lasso and Ruffo Fiesco in Italy and Weelkes and Dowland in England, was pushed further by Vicentino in a treatise of the year 1555 which describes his invention of an instrument in which every tone was divided into five parts. A quarter-tone instrument had already been invented by Zarlino. It is entertaining to note that one Sarti accused Mozart of atonality: 'He is a sectary of the false system that divides the octave into twelve equal semitones, a system sufficiently well known to intelligent artists, and one proved false by harmonic science.' (Ernest Newman, *A Musical Critic's Holiday*.)

## Universality of an Idiom

The above consideration carries with it a corollary that a genuine idiom will be a general feature and not personal or confined to very small groups. It is a common possession and broad enough to permit personal vocabulary to a composer. How does such a phenomenon as the polytonality of certain modern French composers stand in relation to this? Much polytonal writing is only notationally so, chords and key signatures being so manipulated that only one genuine tonality is really employed. There is much more difference of tonality

between the right hand and the left hand in the passage beginning at bar 113 in Schubert's 'Wanderer' Fantasia than in
many alleged modern examples of this device. One suspects,
too, that this device—for I shall not dignify it with the name
of idiom—is not very deeply rooted in the past and does not
arise out of a general tendency, nor a personal emotional
necessity. It is the result of intellectual exercise rather than of
musical impulse, but that in itself need not prevent its being
a medium capable of beauty. Where much of this polytonal
music conveys some clear impression of beauty it seems to
do so in virtue of some momentary harmonic point which is
not an essential feature of polytonality, and which might be
obtained by a more normal technique with much greater
surety.[1]

However, polytonality seems to me to involve a confusion
of idioms. I shall try to explain my point thus. The sense of a
particular tonality is an 'absorbing' sense—it confines—and
does not permit much more impression of alien tonality than
that which the chauvinist has of foreigners. A succession of
notes persistently outside a tonality are just 'out there'. It
requires an exceedingly simple musical content, even accept-
ing the 'out there' relationship, to be able to pay attention to
both streams (to speak here of merely dual tonality). This, of
course, is the explanation of the comparative simplicity of
much polytonal writing which one observes in the lineal layout. How often is not the left hand merely playing an *ostinato*
accompaniment?

It is when a new idiom is both universal, that is to say
capable of appeal to persons nourished by the broad stream

[1] These remarks do not apply to the illustrious French composers Honegger and Milhaud (see chapter on Bartok).

of musical evolution, and persistently explored by a composer of genius and sincerity, that music becomes permanently enriched. In our own time this has been done by Sibelius. Listening to his music one perceives that Sibelius is not concerned to exploit fresh harmonic or rhythmic devices (indeed his harmony is quite old-fashioned), but to write music which is in contact with external nature rather than psychological states, and to do this at once directly and evocatively. Especially this is so in his developments which, I think, are admirably described by a sentence Mr. Ralph Bates applies to Schubert: 'Development is not complex elaboration but *evocation.*'

Sibelius, indeed, is not an outstanding case of inventiveness. He is less inventive than Beethoven, who was always explosively driving along new paths of exploration. The Finnish master's music is great because of its unflinching integrity and its sheer musical quality rather than for the introduction of fresh devices. In this, I feel, he reminds one of Purcell (and, one may add, of our own Vaugham Williams, Bax and Walton). It is true that Purcell's music is distinguished by a very individual line, by the use of established harmonies in new contexts, but it is his marvellous melodic wealth, and above all the breadth, the almost nostalgic melancholy, the tension of much of his music which I feel to be most characteristic of him. His musical devices seem to serve Purcell as a tightrope walker is served by his parasol. It helps him to keep equilibrium, but it is not essential. His music is above devices, it is the most musical of music.

And finally, the quotations at the head of this chapter will serve to show how much the general attitude towards music has changed since the Middle Ages. Yet we may not suppose that Johannes Tinctoris or Simon Tunstede judged music by any other than musical standards. Music might have put to flight the Devil, but no doubt it could do that all the better for being good music. And even if we think that much modern music is designed rather to flatter Baal or the golden calf than to conjure God we ought to bring to it strictly musical criteria. Not the greatest excellence of workmanship nor the smuggest congruity with modern tendencies can justify music that is unfelt by the composer. We may, of course, object to the extensions of musical feeling, yet if we have doubts about the possibilities Mr. Ernest Newman reassures us:

'Future eyes will see, better than we can do, in how narrow a circle of feeling and thought the music of the last thirty years has lived and moved and had its being. The truth, I suppose, is that the human mind—even the collective mind of a civilization—can tackle only one of two big problems at a time, and that three centuries being to the history of music hardly more than a year in the life of an individual, what we have seen since the late sixteenth century is merely an attempt on the part of the general human consciousness to obtain command of a few of the more fundamental musical emotions, and of the simpler means of expressing them. But there must be vast tracks of psychology still almost untouched upon by music and subtleties of musical speech of which even the greatest of our forefathers had no anticipation.'

# Part II: The Performer

★

Auf welches Instrument sind wir gespannt
Und welcher Spieler hat uns in der Hand.
RAINER MARIA RILKE

# Introduction

It may be thought strange that a pianist should consider it in some ways unfortunate that the piano has come to be the instrument most frequently chosen for study by amateur musicians. Yet the fact that it is essentially a solo instrument tends to confine the music lover to what is after all a comparatively narrow realm of musical literature. It is the piano's very capacity which makes of it a danger to catholicity of knowledge. And this is fatal to an art in which narrowness and temporal confinement are anathema to its vital essence.

Indeed, too insistent a preoccupation with externals such as notes and fingers may even hinder one's understanding of music actually written for the pianoforte. It is true that the composer will not succeed in writing great pianoforte music unless he bears in mind the facts of pianoforte technique and tone. But students should remember that the composer does not necessarily conceive his music in relation to the keyboard. To some extent he feels, hears and then plans it in an abstract way. This is discernible in many of the later Beethoven sonatas where, because of the restricted compass of the contemporary instrument a new pianistic style was evolved.

It is this stream of pure creative impulse which a student

should try to follow, without exhausting his attention entirely in the externals of performance. When the study of music is viewed in this way it follows that the pianist's participation in all forms of music-making is imperative. Only in this way can be fostered the necessary flexibility of mind, the ability to grasp and enter the inward musical entity of a composition.

The piano student *must* persuade his friends who play other instruments to join with him in the performance of every kind of chamber work and concerto. He must also attempt to play through the vocal scores of the most famous operas. This procedure has been the essence of my own musical education, and it is impossible to say how much I owe to it.

In another way the mechanical limitations of the piano also stand in the way of the musician's approach to the core of the music he is playing. Once a key is depressed and the hammer has set the string in vibration the player loses all contact with the continued making of the sound. This is a defect which many pianists make worse by not troubling to hold down the key at all after depressing it, trusting to the pedal to carry on the sound, so losing not only physical contact between the sequence of notes but mental and emotional contact also. It is here that the stringed instruments have an immense advantage. (See lesson on Debussy.)

# CHAPTER III

# Technique the Servant of Emotion

. . . E quelli che la musica ci fanno 'vedere' e 'toccare' e ci consentono di 'goderla'.—LUIGI COLONNA.

## The Art of Interpretation

The secret of how to approach and how to prepare and master the interpretation and technique of a piece will be found *in* that piece. There is no need to bring anything to it from outside. All that is necessary is to achieve, by that art of mental appropriation spoken of elsewhere in this book, a knowledge of what the music should sound like in the ideal state. If that mental picture or pattern or idea is concentrated upon, the student will find that he really has an ideal standard with which to compare his playing. Such musical intuitions, or visions, are intermittent and fugitive, and they can be driven away or destroyed by concession to lower standards; yet I believe that the secret of musical appreciation does indeed lie in this contemplative or rather penetrative power of the mind to discipline the physical equipment of the pianist. It is as if the Platonic Ideals really did exist and the mind had power to relate itself to them by effort, and to compare its work with Ideal Beauty.

## *Technique and Rhythm*

The hands are the servants of the mind, and the mind should be supreme in directing them. Mental tension contributes to a stiffening of the muscles, and there cannot be a true relaxation of the arms and hands where there is fear and insecurity in the mind of the artist. There are two principal types of technical difficulties in the art of playing, rhythmical and muscular. It is my experience that all difficulties arise from the fact that one is not always in complete rhythmical command. These technical difficulties grow less if the fundamental and 'inside' rhythm of the music is adhered to. This rhythmic steadiness and poise gives a balance that prevents the muscles from tightening up.

If in playing a passage one listens for two sounds to come together, if one *thinks* them together at that moment, then they will come together. One will be listening to the *time-places* of the notes, and therefore, because the mind will be concentrated on the music itself, there will be no apprehension as to whether the passage can be played or not. The muscles will not be contorted by nervous strain or by the effort of hurrying them or retarding them, of trying to gather up or brace the rhythm.

## *Durations*

Too many people forget that the music is a CONTINUOUS SOUND in the composer's mind. The string player with his bow, the singer, wind or brass player in breathing, can sustain this sound to the end of the composer's intention; but the pianist too often depends on holding the pedal down to keep the sound vibrating, or even if keeping the keys down with the fingers and hands, he loses, through lack of concentration, the mental continuation of the sound which went singing on in the composer's mind. I would, therefore, suggest to pianists, and indeed all players, that they should pay the greatest attention to the lengths and durations of the notes they play and remember as Mozart said, that 'The rests are as important, or even more so, in my music, than the actual notes'. This is the true skeleton on which to build.

## On Slow Music

It is imperative for the sake of the structure and nobility of the line that absolute perfection of rhythm be maintained in performing slow music; this is even more vital than when playing quickly and is a very important point to be remembered, for faults in rhythm (fundamental rhythm, not just tempo) have a way of standing out in a glaring and conspicuous manner. Therefore, it is in slow music that the pianist shows whether or not he is an artist.

In performing quiet pieces he must be just as alert and full of awareness as in the more brilliant and stirring ones. In fact, for this very reason, the right quality and length of every sound, are all the more important. Slackness of line, or a blurred edge, is often caused by a lack of tension or nervous intensity. This tension and awareness must not be of the arms and hands, the muscles of which should be relaxed to get the gentle tone required, but of the spirit.

'The purely technical aspects of playing should be approached through imaginative evocation. Not a scale should be played without some kind of musical intention behind it. And in chord-playing, no clumps of notes! I have always opposed the right-hand, left-hand school of thought. That kind of practising cuts across musical meaning. Surely Bach and Mozart never composed in terms of right and left hands. They simply thought of MUSIC, weaving tones into a single integral pattern, regardless of the mechanics of performance. This pattern, and the meaning behind it, must come through: little hammer-like gestures of right-hand, left-hand, break its flow. Part-thinking, if not part-playing, must be present in every chord. Learn to think in terms of musical pattern and the hands will adjust themselves. The best proof of the power of mind over hands is that once you know exactly how you wish a passage to go, once you hear it right in your head, your fingers will somehow follow your intention and bring your meaning out for you.

'Train yourself to think of music as an expression of life—not merely a pattern of habits and actions, but the actual pulse and breath of life. For life itself has its own pulse, its own beat. Waking or sleeping, our breathing has its individual rhythm. Sometimes that rhythm is varied by our emotions, larger-scaled varieties occurring through long-rooted habits of blood or nationality. That the Germanic pulse-beat is somewhat slower than the Latin, is revealed by its language as well as its music. It is a part of musical interpretation to recognize this all-over pulse beat (a quite different thing from the marked rhythm of the piece) and to reflect it faithfully. Learn the rhythm of the age that produced a given work. Do not play Bach, Beethoven, Schumann, with a twentieth-century pulse beat.'[1]

[1] Reprinted from a conference in *Étude*, The Music Magazine, with Rose Heylbut, copyright 1948 by the Theodore Presser Co.

I want to express my beliefs concerning the much debated question of Relaxation and Exertion.

## Rapid Alternation of Relaxation and Exertion

I do not agree with that school of teaching that advocates entire muscular relaxation, nor do I find that continued exertion (pressing the key down after the hammer has hit the string) is any better. Balance of the muscles (as obtained, for instance, by the Japanese and Greek Equilibrists who can do incredible feats of balancing) depends not so much upon relaxation or exertion but upon the scientific *combination* of both these opposites, and not only must this combination be considered but every muscle must be used relatively to the others. That is what is known as poise. So that even a third school which might insist that one set of muscles, shall we say those of the arm, should be quite relaxed, while another, perhaps those of the hand, should be in violent exertion, is hardly right. I insist that not only should the hand and the muscles of the arm work in relation to one another, but that there should be a combination of relaxation and exertion in all the muscles of the body. The secret of poise and freedom is a *holding together* of relaxation and exertion, the one coming fast upon the other at a tremendous rate.

## Rotary Action

When passages are being played involving rotary exertion each consecutive note is played with the opposite side of the hand to that used for the preceding note; it therefore stands to reason that in playing towards the right one must exert the muscles of the hand towards the right, and similarly, in playing towards the left one must exert the muscles towards the left. It follows from this that when one set of muscles has been used it should be immediately relaxed, so that the hand is free to 'exert' in the opposite direction. Failure to do this will involve the muscles in a virtual tug-o'-war, to the loss of all charm and fluidity in the music. It will not be necessary for those who have a good stretch to move the hand about from side to side too much. I approve more of rotary freedom than of rotary action, and I advise the latter only if there is any danger of stiffening the muscles.[1]

## On Touch

Sir James Jeans in his book, *Science and Music*, says that the greatest virtuoso, as long as he confines himself to striking single notes, has no greater range of effects at his disposal than a child strumming at its five-finger exercise, although many pianists are firmly convinced that they can put a vast amount of expression in the striking of a single note on the piano: they even claim to be able to draw the whole gamut of emotion out of a single key. The untemperamental scientist, as Sir James calls himself, points out that in striking a single note the pianist has only one variable at his disposal—the force with which he strikes the key. This determines the velocity with which the hammer hits the strings and, once this is settled, all the rest follows automatically. It is not, however, a legitimate inference—he tells us—that single notes can differ only in loudness. Differences in the strength of striking will also produce a difference in the proportion in which the various har-

[1] See *Relaxation Studies* by Tobias Matthay.

monics enter and this will naturally alter the emotional quality of the note.

There are technical considerations which will enable one to get varying qualities of tone. For a piercingly beautiful singing tone, the student does not have to press the key right down as far as it will go to enable the hammer to start moving. Sound is produced at the point when the key is roughly four-fifths of the way down to the key bed. Now, by not putting the key down too far the player leaves the hammer more free to hit the string in such a way as to enable it to vibrate very quickly. The resultant freedom of vibration gives a very intense quality to the singing tone. Using this manner of producing sound the student will have to learn to make an accurate judgement of the depth to which the key must be depressed and also to adjust the speed at which it is depressed. The key must indeed descend rather quickly, otherwise the tone will be too soft.

I use the same kind of key action when playing Debussy, because that composer also needs the sound of many vibrations, but as his pieces are more nebulous than Chopin's I do not move the key so quickly. Not only must the pianist concentrate on how he moves the key, but he must be aware at the identical moment of how the hammer should hit the string. However impossible it may seem at the commencement, continued experiment will give quite surprising results in the way of tonal variety.

When we consider the tone of a certain pianist as being very individual and special, when we think we recognize his touch, it is because we are listening to an emotional quality consciously achieved by the differing strengths in which this artist strikes the key. Of course, every pianist plays with varying strengths of tone, according to the demands of dynamics indicated by the line of the composer, which he should follow faithfully. But even with the limits of *forte* and *piano*, one pianist will never use the same set of strengths as another. It is not only his own personal reading of the work that affects his muscular action, but his whole psychological and physical make-up is involved.

When Sir James Jeans asked me what I thought about his theory, I told him I agreed with him almost unreservedly, but that different pianists did seem to give an illusory impression of differing touch, as explained above, and I pointed out to him that not only did I think the emotional quality, as he described it, affected the strength of the striking of a note, but that quite ordinary physical attributes might have their part. For instance, if the pianist sits forward he strikes the key more speedily. If he sits back, his fingers will not be so bent, and the weight of the arm will be more behind the flat finger, thus causing the key to be depressed more slowly, and the tone will be rounder and softer in quality. I suggested, too, that many people when they talk of 'touch' or 'tone' really mean 'style', and that would include those idiosyncracies for which some players are noted, such as hurrying when the music gets louder, and slowing up when the music gets softer, the slackening up before the first chord of the bar, or the hastening at the end. Some pianists seem naturally to adopt a non-*legato* way of playing semiquaver passages even if the musical line is lyrical and requires a *cantabile* tone.

## *Memorization*

Upon the mental side, one's performance of music un-doubtedly gains purity and approaches the ideal beauty more closely if one memorizes the score. I have long thought that a musical memory is very much a physical attribute. A musical memory should not be confused with the ability to reproduce music on an instrument without a copy. One of the most important factors in the latter gift is the sense of Relative Pitch. I know several people who come to a stop when performing from memory, not because they forget the music, in fact they are quite well able to sing the rest of the piece, but simply because they do not possess the gift of Manual Relative Pitch, and cannot associate what they hear in their heads with its position on the keyboard or strings; in other words they cannot blindly find their way. It is very difficult for me to explain this, as I believe it has never before been touched upon and the word 'memory' is used loosely to cover diverse phenomena, but I have always been very interested in observing this fact. Frequently some of my really *unmusical* pupils have been able to play to me from memory almost at once, and especially to 'play by ear' whereas I have had pupils possessing really genuine musical ability and comprehension who have been unable to play from memory without the greatest difficulty, although they knew and carried all the sounds in their heads. This type of person has to rely very largely upon repeated practice in order to get first of all a kind of automatic placing and spacing of the fingers on the keyboard. This is what I call 'finger memory' and in my own case I depend very much upon it.

One has to examine and study in every possible aspect and detail the structure, scheme of modulation, harmonies, and so on, of a piece of music in the course of one's ordinary work of interpretation of it; that is one has to understand what the composer MEANS: what he has to SAY in the work. Thus deep association, familiarity with and contemplation of a work must inevitably assist in memorizing it.

Some people possess the faculty of visualizing the printed page, and for many others this may serve as a general guide. The student should by self-analysis discover what type of memory he possesses and make his effort of retention accordingly.

With the foregoing in mind, I am sure the student will be ready to approach the compositions which I have chosen for study in Part III of this Book.

## On Great Pianists

It is inevitable that a pianist should be asked to name the greatest pianists of the past age and to give reasons for his choice. In selecting Rachmaninoff, Paderewski and Busoni (alas, I was too young to have heard of Raoul Pugno) I have done so because they played as if they were the creators of the work they were performing. They have, as it were, got 'under the skin' of the composer. It is for this reason that Paderewski's performance of the first movement of the Chopin B Flat Minor Sonata is so unforgettable: music which I have always thought inspired Wagner in parts of the 'Walküre'. The great crashing chords, in their upward or downward sweep, were like mountainous waves, breaking and receding. The contrapuntal line was laid aside for the harmonic.

It seems a paradoxical thing to say, but Paderewski appeared to be thinking of the music orchestrally. In Chopin's later works, such as the Sonatas and the Barcarolle, the progress of the music is increasingly orchestral and harmonic and he seems partially to have abandoned the merely pianistic technical devices of his earlier works. I would advise all pianists who aspire to play modern music, whether it be Bartok or Britten, Bloch or Hindemith, to study the Barcarolle of Chopin, to enable them to compass the change of style required.

Paderewski succeeded in re-creating the IDEA of the composer in spite of many mistakes and omissions. The ensemble between the two hands was not always very good. Sometimes his tone was hard. Sometimes he over-exaggerated the nuances of tempo. But his vision of the composer's idea was so strong and so revealing that one didn't hear any of the mistakes at the time, and it was only on analysis, after the concert, that one was aware of them, and, rightly, dismissed them.

Rachmaninoff, in his performance of the last movement of the Chopin B Flat Minor Sonata, revolutionized the usual interpretation. Every pianist of the day who heard him said that never before had the finale been played like that. In his striving to understand what the composer was trying to express, he listened anew to the music, casting off all prejudice and partiality, and even all memory, and listened 'creatively' as it were. He played it with the freshness of one who might have composed it. This movement, which had served as a vehicle to show off the performer at his speediest and most fluent, became under Rachmaninoff's fingers, an urgent series of harmonies set in rhythms that seemed mysterious and new, but were the true accents and dynamics as conceived by the composer. Being possessed of the greatest technique one had ever heard, paradoxically technique meant nothing to him, except as a means to an end, and such importance did he give to each and every individual note, that his playing had a great sense of deliberation about it.

Therefore, it is these interpretations of the Chopin B Flat Minor Sonata by Rachmaninoff and Paderewski that aid me in my effort to get 'under the skin' of the composer. I will name as supreme in piano playing the performances of Busoni of the Beethoven Concertos, and the latest Sonatas, performances of such Olympian greatness that Plato if he had heard them might have added them as a rung to the Ladder of Beauty in his symposium.

Busoni was a supreme architect of piano music, and of the three I believe him to have been the greatest. When I heard him play, I forgot the keyboard completely. He took music away from the realm of interpretation into the rarer climates of re-creation. His playing of the Beethoven Concerto in E♭ Major, although evanescent for us like all musical performances that are not recorded on the gramophone, is not really lost to us now. It belongs to all time, and is as enduringly beautiful in memory as the golden vision of the Parthenon. Indeed whenever I heard Busoni playing the slow movement of this Concerto I always thought of the pure and simple lines of this Greek Temple. Both Beethoven and Phideas possessed an equally calm and perfect simplicity of line.

Inspired as Busoni was, his technical control was marvellous, and he used his hands as a precision tool to enable him to fashion the rhythm, colour and line to perfection.

Varying ways of interpreting a work are usual and expected. The executant, even when faithfully trying to reproduce the composer's original intention, cannot help expressing his own personality, though his feelings are held in control. His temperament, experience, even his desires and needs, are bound to affect the original matrix. I have heard completely opposite interpretations of the same work, both sincere, and deeply felt, and both satisfactory; but Inspiration cannot occur twice, and, in interpretation, one should try to evoke that moment when the work was conceived within the composer's mind, thus to rest for all time as the true model and standard for performance.

# Part III: The Technique of the Approach to Music

★

There will nothing conduce more to ye perfect ataining to play on ye harpsichord or spinnet, than a serious application to ye following rules.— HENRY PURCELL, Introduction to *Musick's Hand-Maid*.

# *Foreword*

By far the most satisfactory way of developing a student's
musical sensibilities is jointly to study with him a composition,
analysing it from the standpoint of the player whose task it is
to exhibit its beauty at its fullest. It is for this reason that I
have written the *lessons* which follow. Generalizations about
the manner of playing Bach, Mozart or Chopin may be of
value but they are apt to prove useless to the student when he
sits down to the piano before an individual composition. And
it is in order to help the student to understand his duty towards the modern composer that I preface the lessons that
end my book with the brief study of the relationship between
the public and the creative artist from which the student will
learn where he stands as the interpreter of both.

It is regrettable that he seems reluctant to learn contemporary
music even when he is interested in it, feeling no doubt that
it would be wasted in his future career, the public seemingly
not wanting to hear anything later than the music of the nine-

teenth century. In building up his repertory the student should continually widen his horizon and not confine his studies solely to the music of the classics. He will perceive then that there is no essential difference between contemporary and other music. Music, which is for all time, is always contemporary. One finds as crude outbursts in Byrd and Beethoven as in Stravinsky, when something of the same emotion demands it.


## CONTEMPORARY ART

Now lies the earth all Danaë to the stars
And all thy heart lies open unto me.
ALFRED LORD TENNYSON.

### The Public

I have the fanciful idea that the relationship between the creative artist and the public is a kind of Barmecide Feast in the Persian manner. The public (or diners) are present, but only as onlookers and the meal is eaten *for* them, the idea being that they should thus savour all the more exquisitely the vicarious repast. In other words, it is they who, through the artist, create the music they hear, paint the pictures they see, and write the books they read. When a sensitive member of the general public listens to 'Le Roi David' of Honegger, or looks at a painting by Matisse, he often feels these works of art to be a part of him. At some time he may have experienced the same vibration, the same urgent need to express what has happened on the canvas or full score. He, too, has felt like that. The composer, the artist, is the 'ghost', as it were, who has created these works of art on his behalf.

# The Artist

I have said in an earlier chapter that the composer transforms the emotion of the communal mind: he expresses the quintessence of the emotion of the day. In the general way it is what is in the air that comes to a head in a certain artist, be he painter, composer or writer.

This is certainly true of Beethoven who was nineteen or twenty years of age when the French Revolution broke out. But revolution had been in the air for decades. Such revolts do not occur from one moment to the next; they simmer and swell for years before. What was in the air must have affected him; if ever there was a revolutionary artist it was he.

Similarly, are not the great battle pictures of the Spanish painter Goya the outcome of the Napoleonic wars, a tremendous taking sides with the oppressed? They are socialistic, anti-clerical, in just the same way as those of Picasso are to-day.

There is, of course, in this 'something in the air' affecting artists, a paradox—for it is often the artist who evokes this new condition that permeates the creative world. Smetana, the ardent Bohemian, was able to thrill his fellow-countrymen, the then vassals of Austro-Hungarian Emperors, to mad fervour with his patriotic music. I cannot imagine that any Czech could hear 'Ma Vlast' (My Country) and not be stirred to the very depths, and roused to fight for the freedom of his people.

And such was the lively patriotism of Clavé, the Catalan workman, who revived the Catalan language with his Orfeon Choir, that it is said the feeling for a Separatist Catalonia was revivified by the singing in the Catalan language of this marvellous group of singers.

All art is spiritually a reflection of the age which produces it. Just as Bach breathed some of the fervour of the Reformation and Beethoven was permeated with the 'awareness' of nature which characterized the era in which he lived, so Modigliani, the 'modern Raphael' as some describe him, reflects the spirit of the twentieth century in his enormous influence on contemporary architecture, engineering, etc.—an influence which resulted in Streamline and created the idea of the modern woman with her attentuated figure, haunting melancholy face, strange hairdressing and clothes. Thus the artist is inspired by and himself inspires the stream of history in which he lives. W. B. Yeats put it this way:

> *Our towns are copied fragments from our breasts*
> *And all man's Babylons strive but to impart*
> *The grandeurs of his Babylonian heart.*

# CHAPTER IV

# Elizabethan Keyboard Music by Byrd, Gibbons, Bull and Clarke

Like gold to aery thinness beaten.—JOHN DONNE.

It is amazing that there are still musically minded people who are unacquainted with the wealth of loveliness which the Elizabethan age produced. Yet it is true that this period actually provides the very foundations of keyboard art. The history of this foundation is still in part obscure but there can be no doubting that it occurred. For instance, there exists some fourteenth-century English organ music of which one of the pieces is chiefly harmonized in consecutive fifths. They are, however, really accompaniments to vocal music. After this there is only one piece until the early Tudor period, and then music is already considerably developed in the music of such as Tallis and Taverner and Radford. Secular keyboard music was of course later in making its first appearance, but when it does it already possesses considerable richness. Vocal music was often transferred directly as written to the viols and lute as we know from the prefaces to various collections of music such as Dowland's *First Book of Ayres* (1591) which are 'so made that all the parts together, or either of them severally, may be sung to Lute, Orpharion or Viol de Gambo'.

The virginals were not used as voice-accompanying instruments, but the song tradition is seen quite clearly in the variations form which was probably originated by William Byrd, or at least applied to the keyboard. It is a form which he handled extremely well, so that later composers, including Schubert in the D Minor quartet, used some of his devices, notably that of simply restating the theme at the close. Great floridity developed and this was transferred to church music, so that like Bishop Cyrilo Franco, Cranmer was moved to protest against music that was 'stuffed full of notes'. It is a complaint we meet again made by Joseph II of Austria against the work he had commissioned from Mozart.

Yet although superficiality and monotony can be found in those lovely collections, the Queen Elizabeth Virginal Book, the Cosyn Virginal Book, the Lady Neville Book and others, there is about the music of this period a rare spirituality which is best indicated by the quotation from Donne which I have placed at the head of this chapter.

These pieces require the utmost simplicity of style. Though technically they are comparatively easy, they are, because of their simple artlessness, fragrance and innocent perfection, amongst the hardest pieces in the repertory of the keyboard.

In the slow pieces there should be a *still* quality in the playing. After the rich harmonies of the latter-day composers, the Elizabethan music may seem a little bare and the chords empty. But this is really one of its greatest charms, for the actual sound itself will seem more definable, and the very changes in the vibrations of sound will therefore become momentous. The ensemble between the hands must be perfect and the pedal must be used very sparingly, if at all. The very greatest attention must be paid to the task of keeping clear the outline of each part.

Many editors of these old pieces differ as to whether the ornaments with which the old manuscripts abounded should be played on the modern piano or not. Those who think they should be omitted say that (1) they were a speciality of virginals technique and are now obsolete; (2) they may frequently be the inaccurate additions of copyists; (3) their interpretation is uncertain, even experts disagreeing. I personally think that the very early keyboard music is complete without ornaments, but that the later period needs them: in this I am guided by my musical feeling, accordingly in the following lesson the ornaments are omitted in the works of William Byrd, John Bull, Orlando Gibbons, but in the *Jigg* of Jeremiah Clarke the ornaments remain, being written out in full in the present edition.

### PAVANA BY WILLIAM BYRD[1]

William Byrd, who was born about 1541, was the greatest composer of his time in the whole world, and the greatest English composer, with the exception of Purcell and Elgar, until this very day, when men like Vaughan Williams and Arnold Bax carry on his great tradition. There are two pieces dedicated to me by these composers, the *Hymn-Tune Prelude* of Vaughan Williams and the *Mountain Mood* of Arnold Bax, which might have been written by a modern William Byrd.

The time signature C/3 means that there are three semibreves in a bar (equivalent to our modern time signature of

[1] Augener Ltd.

3/2=3 minims). The C is a survival of the division of the breve into two semibreves, and the three implies the dividing of the breves into three. It must be remembered throughout that whereas a Galliardo is an Elizabethan dance of gay and yet 'knightly' character, the Pavane which generally precedes it is of a slower and and statelier character.

All three notes of the first chord of this piece should be played out equally, the melody being carried on with the lower part in the left hand, and the bar continued in that manner. In the second bar, the top part should be separated from the other two parts, letting it sing out plaintively, the other two parts being quiet. In bar 3, the middle part in the R.H. takes over the motive still more strongly. The E major chord in bar 4 is played *subito piano*, with an infinitesimal comma before the chord. Generally the fingering is within the natural stretch of the hand, but sometimes it will be necessary to use a thumb or finger twice, and especial care must be taken to keep as much as possible on the keyboard by adopting a sliding manner of hand movement. For instance, in bar 2, fourth finger on B in the R.H., top part, must slide on to C, while in bar 5, R.H. top part, the fifth on D must slide to E.

In the next few bars the most prominent part is in the R.H. I agree with the editor's suggestions as to *crescendo* and *forte*, but these must be done on a very small scale. A clear, rather cold tone is what is required. In bar 8, the top part D should even sound a little shrill, like a trumpet. In bars 6, 7 and 8, the L.H. should be kept rather quiet, in spite of the *crescendo* in the R.H. In bars 7–8 there is a charming alternation of D minor and D major—this *tierce de picardie* is a device frequently used by the Elizabethan composers. It is to be found in all these pieces.

The second part is begun rather more boldly. It should not be too *legato*, but there should be a ringing quality in the tone. To get the right spirit it will help to think of the time being divided by 2 instead of 3, i.e. the bars should be regarded as containing one dotted minim, and three separate crotchets. What has been said previously about the rhythm of Elizabethan music must be borne in mind here, for the barring has had to be left very much to the modern editor. The A in bar 11 should be emphasized. G.F.E. imitates the preceding bar in the R.H. From that bar a *diminuendo* should be made.

As an instance of this freedom in barring, bar 14 should really be one of four minims, the next bar line occurring before the second beat of bar 15. Musical instinct will indicate where the phrasing and therefore the barring lies. One should think of the musical accent and forget the bar line.

### ALMAN BY JOHN BULL[1]

The *Alman*, perhaps better known by its French name of *Allemande*, is one of the dances of the suite, and is played moderately quickly. This *Alman* of John Bull should be taken at the time of a rather vigorous march, *Andante* is, in my opinion, too slow. The phrase marks must be regarded purely as such, nor should one forget the overlapping parts in the L.H., such as in bar 4, where the lower part imitates the top part of the bar before carrying on into bar 5.

Here again a rather shrill 'trumpet call' tone must be used for the first phrase of six bars. The repeat or variation (Bach called it Double) is to be played quietly, using *portamento* in the R.H. (in this type of piece I mean by *portamento* a *separate-*

[1] Joseph Williams.

*ness in legato*), but the shrill non-*portamento* touch should be retrieved at the end of the phrase, in bars (end of) 10, 11, 12. The first part, of course, must be played in a very rhythmical manner.

## The Second Part

*Maestoso* should apply to the manner and not to the *tempo* of this section, which should be well accented. The phrase which starts at the end of bar 15 must be played very lightly and softly (*portamento*). The next phrase, which starts at the end of bar 17, should be played *cantabile*, *legato*, with a *crescendo* and the very slightest broadening of the time towards the G major chord and this should be the only *nuance* of *tempo* during the whole piece. From the end of bar 19 quiet and moderate playing must prevail until the end of the phrase in bar 23. It is not necessary to play repeats as they are only a variation of the principal theme. In this *Alman* I do not play the repeat of the second part as I think it is very uninspiring but, on the other hand, I repeat the music from bars 13 to 23.

## CORANTO BY ORLANDO GIBBONS[1]

A *Coranto* is a quick running dance, and was also one of the dances of the suite. In spite of the plaintive quality of the melody, this *Coranto* should be kept moving along. The first three bars must be phrased towards the fourth bar, where the next phrase, which closes at the end of bar 6, begins. The music so far makes one long phrase, itself containing two long and one short phrases. The next long phrase also contains three

[1] Joseph Williams.

smaller ones, one long, one short, and one long, the first of
which must be begun with a singing quality in the R.H.
while the L.H. plays very softly, the tone following the line
of the phrase. There will be a slight *diminuendo* towards the
fourth bar, coming up again as marked, and then one must
start bar 7 very quietly, forgetting the next two bar lines and
playing straight towards bar 10. The marked *crescendo* must
sing out plaintively, while the bass should receive due prominence, as in bars 8 and 11, the other parts in the L.H. being kept
very quiet. It is imperative that a very audible *diminuendo*
should be heard in the phrase at the end of bar 10 and this
ought to continue to the beginning of bar 13, where a singing
*crescendo* and *vibrato* should occur with a further *crescendo*
towards bar 14. The F in the bass of bar 14 must be well
marked. Here a *subito diminuendo* in the L.H. will leave the
R.H. singing quietly, after which a *diminuendo* to bar 16 must
be made. I always repeat the first part of the *Coranto* for the
lovely intial tune does not come again. I begin the repeat
*pianissimo*, using the same nuances but on a much smaller
scale. One thing the student must remember to do is to keep
the whole thing moving, through every shade of nuance and
variation of tone.

## The Second Part

The second part should be played *mezzo-piano* in both
hands, without distinction between the parts, but falling away
a little in tone at the end of bar 19 and beginning of 20. If
this first phrase is begun in rather an expressionless manner, it
will bring into more marked relief the lovely melody and
harmony of the first part. One should start bar 21 very quietly,

using thumb on G in R.H. and making a *crescendo* as indicated but in both hands, keeping the tone up to the C major chord in bar 24. The second and third crotchets in the L.H. must be played very quietly in that bar. A good fingering for bar 25 is this:

The *crescendo* should be played as marked, but in the next bars it is good to make the *diminuendo* two notes sooner as this gives a broader curve to the phrase. A warm tone pervades bars 25 and 26, L.H. while from bar 29 the melody must sing out softly in the R.H., the L.H. being kept very quiet except for a little emphasis on the bass notes. In bar 23 one must, contrary to the first part, make a *diminuendo*, the whole piece getting softer and making a *calando* to the very end of the piece. The bass note F at the end of bar 24 must be sounded clearly with a little nuance of tone in bar 35. Played thus the dynamic graduation is from *piano* to *pianissimo*.

### JIGG BY JEREMIAH CLARKE[1]

Mr. Jerry Clarke, as he was called, is said to have been born in 1669. His name occurs in the Chapel Royal list as a pupil of Dr. Blow. The great Henry Purcell too was a pupil of Dr. Blow. Dr. Clarke also wrote for the spinet and harpsichord as well as for the virginals.

This little Jigg is written in the form of an interrupted canon. By interrupted canon I mean the canon goes on for about two bars and then the second part, instead of

[1] J. & W. Chester, Ltd.

exactly copying the first part, goes off on its own for a bar or more as the case may be. Apart from the accents marked in the copy remember that, in a piece like this, the Durations are of the utmost importance. Failure to observe this will result in unrhythmical and unsteady playing, especially in the first part. It will be observed that while one hand is playing quavers the other is playing a crotchet and a quaver, or semi-quavers, and if the same amount of tone is given to the different durations of notes, this will throw the rhythm out. In turn this will result in a tendency to run away with the music, involving by reaction a stiffening of the muscles in order to assert control. Thus each fault will lead to a worse one.

The reason the editor marked the second and fourth notes of the first bar *staccato* was to draw attention to the Durations. It is quite enough if one plays the quavers naturally lighter than the crotchets. (The second crotchet in bar 2, L.H. is a misprint for a quaver.) In a piece as quick as this I advise the playing of the ornaments in the R.H. with the beat in the L.H. Indeed, I wonder if the grace notes in bar 5, R.H. were added by a copyist after the composer's death, for they do not seem natural to him. It is advisable to leave them out or to substitute an inverted mordent, which was probably what he meant. The whole should be played with a bright *mezzo-forte* tone, in a lively manner, accented, but not too heavily, with the greatest rhythm and sparkle.


*Variations in the Canon*

In the fourth bar, L.H. as elsewhere instead of continuing the canon goes off of its own sweet will. In bar 3 a little prominence in the L.H. is needed, while in bar 4 the R.H.

gradually comes into its own again, until in bar 5 it starts a new canon. In bar 6, R.H., I use fifth finger on semiquaver F♯, and in the L.H. change thumb to fourth finger on the second E. It is in these bars that one discovers how difficult it is, without a proper care of Duration, to get the gay rhythmical character that the piece needs. The playing must be controlled but not stiff, for rhythmically difficult music is not controlled with hands and arms, but with brains and ears. In bar 7 the tone must be dropped, especially in R.H., so as to facilitate the initiation of the *crescendo*. In the last phrase (bar 10) the syncopated accent on second quaver must be shown clearly. No pause must occur between the first and second parts.

A more stolid and heavy fashion should characterize the second part, though without exceeding a *mezzo-forte*. In bar 14 I change fourth finger to fifth on the second C♯ in R.H., and in the next bar, third to second on F♯ in L.H. In the next bar the tone must be brought down after the first accent to *piano* and kept to *piano* for the next four bars, except for the accented crotchets which occur in every bar. In the passage marked *diminuendo* the phrasing in the R.H. must be preserved, the L.H. notes being played *staccato*. This gives a charming light quality to the phrase, which should be maintained till the end of the piece in the L.H. A useful fingering for the end of bar 19, 20 in the L.H., is 512/353. The rest of the L.H. to the end of the piece must be played in groups. This will mean using the thumb twice in succession, 151 151, etc. The R.H. must be kept *piano*, the L.H. *pianissimo*, *leggiero*, and *staccato*. From bar 27 it is best to play in a sturdy louder manner and very rhythmically, bar 29 in particular should be well accented on the first of each group. Bar 31, L.H. should be quite detached, but played out *mezzo-forte*. (In my opinion, bar 34 should read the same as the first bar.) I play *pianissimo* in both hands in bar 35 and continue so to the end of the piece, making no pause at the end.

# CHAPTER V

# *Bach*

Musik sei zur Ehre Gottes und zur
Erbauung der Menschheit.

J. S. BACH.

There has always seemed to me to be the closest relation between the inward content of the music of Bach and his position in the history of musical technique. Those who approach
his music with a responsive and receptive mind are often
moved to exclaim against the tradition they have perhaps
heard in their youth that Bach is quite devoid of feeling. That
such a tradition existed is barely credible, nowadays. Yet it
did exist, and I suppose it found its justification in the evident
perfection of Bach's mastery of technique, as if it were argued
that one who displayed such proficiency could not possibly
have been profoundly moved.

It is precisely this absolute sureness of technique which, I
think, enables Bach to be so profoundly moving. The solid
structure of his art, suggesting strength and will and immense
power, is yet filled with a tenderness and pathos which seems
all the more real because of that strength. It is in this sense
that Bach sums up an epoch. Despite the enormous service he
rendered to music by having the boldness to make use of the
well-tempered clavichord, he did not set out to renovate the
technique of counterpoint, but to use it as it stood. He is the
last of the great contrapuntalists.

Similarly one feels, I think, far more than in Handel, that

moving spirit of communal religion which had been awakened by the Reformation, already in decline, and which finds its last profound musical expression in Bach. The difference between these two great composers might almost be said to be that Handel, unlike Bach, seems naturally to turn towards Jehovah, even when he writes of the Messiah. In Bach one feels the man's individual yearning comforted, yet not made self-reliant nor yet betrayed into exultant confidence, by the corporate body of believers around him. The searching and intensely spiritual content of Bach is ecstatic. In a sense he looks back emotionally to the sweeping fervour of the Reformation, as he does technically upon the declining age of polyphony. The whole breadth of the musical tradition is summed up in him, his sources were not local and nationalistic; a German, and with all the weight and strength of the German, he could study the Italians with care and devotion; a Protestant, he could recognize the spiritual drama and the symphonic possibilities of the mass.

CHORAL PRELUDE: 'BELOVED JESU, WE ARE HERE'[1]

Chegai, Chegai, peccador, ao pe da crux Fica Nosso Senhor.

I have talked about the influences at work on Bach, because I think it necessary to understand, and to get into one's playing something of the ecstasy which must have possessed him when he wrote this beautiful Choral Prelude. There must be a mood of elevation in one's playing of such music. So far as the notes are concerned, it is not at all difficult. But it must be played in a very quiet manner, with the melody, that is the Choral, sung out somewhat piercingly, although of course always very soft, and with a melancholy tone.

[1] (Arr. Harriet Cohen). Oxford University Press.

The time must be absolutely precise and even, and there must not be the slightest liberty taken with the rhythm. All the inner parts must move to their appointed places in the quietest possible manner—they must be several shades softer than the Canto—and as smoothly as one can play, even when there are jumps and stretches.

There are some parts which it may be impossible to sustain without the use of the pedal, such as the first beat of the first bar in the left hand. Pianists who cannot stretch nine will have to release the bass G with the finger and leave it to the pedal to sustain.

In places where there are ten one must play the two parts in the left hand as a spread chord, taking care that the pedal has caught the bass part (little finger) before the thumb jumps on to the Tenor Part.

It is an invariable rule for spread chords that one changes the pedal with the lower note and not with the top. It is surprising how many pupils to whom I have given lessons have failed to do this. I also find it unfortunately necessary to remind students that the pedal must be put down immediately *after* a note has been sounded and released as one prepares to strike the next note.

For example:

In this Choral the bars in which great care has to be taken over this spread chord pedalling are 4, 9, 14. In the opening chord it is to be presumed that one will use the 4th or 5th finger on the B in the right hand and silently change to the 3rd finger to permit the playing of the following notes, starting with the 4th or 5th finger, *legato*.

The trill in bar 4 is performed thus:

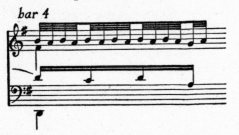

In the second bar, 3rd beat, the Second Part starts on the semiquaver A below middle C. It is difficult to stretch this unless one uses the thumb on two consecutive notes, on the A and B. This facilitates the keeping down of the minim A.

## Use of Thumb in Sustaining Parts

Wherever difficulty is experienced in sustaining the parts because of stretches, the thumb must be used on two consecutive notes, e.g. in bar 3, the bar of the trill, there are two instances of this practice:

One has gently to slide the thumb over the surface of the keys in such cases. The repetition of this first part of the Choral is to be played in the quietest possible manner, deepening, if possible, the sense of reverence.

### Tone of the Choral

After the second double bar the Choral should be made to sing out in the soprano part, but not with a fat, bland kind of tone as would be used in the Chopin E Flat Major Nocturne; it must have a piercing, poignant quality, though never being hard, while all the other parts must be kept quiet and remote. It is of extreme importance to handle the ensemble with absolute precision. Chords must be played with as much simultaneity as a good string quartet uses.

Except in such cases as the first beat of the piece, where one has to hold the pedal down over two beats (I am assuming that students cannot stretch nine in the left hand), the pedal has to be changed with every quaver beat throughout the piece.

At bar 13, the student may again need guidance. At the second beat in the R.H., the melodic line should be carried out in the semiquavers, so:

bar 13

and the next beat must be played very softly. At bar 14, first beat, I take the A in the Tenor with the right hand, so that there are not too many spreads in the bar, thus:

The octave G in bar 15 should be tied to the G in bar 16, the B in the Tenor being the only note sounded in bar 16. Play all three other parts in bar 15 with the right hand.

The piece should now be played in a very broad, *nobilmente* manner, yet without too much increase of tone or too much use of *ritenuto*. I can only liken this breadth to a sort of very deep breathing—a quiet 'bigness'.

### PRELUDES AND FUGUES

> . . . Anthems cleer,
> As may with sweetnes, through mine ear,
> Dissolve me into extasies.
> MILTON, Il Penseroso.

For the Preludes and Fugues of Bach I use an edition of the music which has neither expression marks nor marks of *tempo*—an edition such as that in which Bach's works were first published. My aim in using such an edition is to avoid the intrusion on my mind of any ideas other than those of the composer. The student should try to make an interpretation which will come closest to that which he thinks Bach originally meant. I must impress on him that my own analysis which follows has been built up bar by bar to show the lines on which I study a work, and the interpretation must be regarded as personal, the student being left quite free to express it in his or her own way. I must impress upon him that I do not want him to mimic my own manner of playing.

Interpretation should be the art of representing the composer's own conception of his music, and this one should discover for oneself by careful study of the music. Busoni told me that Bach himself said: 'There is only one way to play my music, and that way the music itself must tell you. If you cannot find out yourself what my music means, you should not play it.' At any rate, he left his music unmarked. Therefore what we all have to learn is to express the composer—his feeling, his ideas, his emotions—not to express ourselves.

Even advanced students will do well to remember Professor Fuller-Maitland's definition of a fugue. 'The Fugue is a composition for several independent 'voices', interwoven according to certain regulations. The *Subject* is stated by one voice or part and followed after an interval by another, keeping the same notes, at a different pitch. The latter is called the *Answer*. The first voice, well imitated by the second, has something different to say, this new material being called the *Counter Subject*. When all the voices have entered they complete what is called the *Exposition* and soon a new series of entries is contrived, usually in a different order, called the *Counter Exposition*.'

He goes on to say that 'the Preludes have no such rigid

plan as the Fugues', they are mostly built on a single musical figure, and in some there is good evidence that they were first intended as technical exercises.

## The Prelude

The question that comes to one's mind on looking at the Prelude is: 'How is one going to get colour by *crescendos* and *diminuendos*, and how balance them, for the Prelude is all built on the same figure, and is not broken up into phrases?' One answer to this is to be found in the harmony. The changes of harmony will tell one when to increase in tone and when to play softly. If one plays the Prelude through as a series of chords one finds that some require softer playing than others.

With this in mind I begin the Prelude very softly, building up a *crescendo* to the fifth bar, *because the harmony calls for it*. Bar 6 brings a drop in tone, this is restored in bar 7 while bars 8, 9 and 10 decline in tone. The harmony from the beginning is moving in one long phrase towards the change to the dominant key in bar 11.

The chord of the twelfth bar is resolved on to an inversion of the D minor chord, therefore that simple common chord of bar 13 must be quieter than the disturbing one in bar 12, the same remarks applying to bars 14 and 15. From bar 16 I begin a *crescendo* which goes on for four bars and which takes us back to the major opening part. Now as in bar 20 we get a new chord, on the same bass note, it is obvious that we must make some sort of difference in tone. Therefore I start that new chord very very softly, and go on piling on tone until the sixth bar from the end. Then I let it all subside until the last chord which I play quite *piano*.

Personally I use the pedal in this Prelude, but it is purely a matter of choice. I change it twice in a bar, namely with each minim.

The greatest care must be taken to keep the semiquavers absolutely even. The hands and arms must be kept very free and loose, for it will be noticed that the semiquaver passages are rapid in time, going from one side of the hand to the other. Thus one is using one set of muscles as one plays to the right side of one's hand and different ones in playing to the left side. Difficulty will be avoided by keeping absolutely free and loose.

### The Fugue

It will be seen that all the four voices come in in the first five bars, in the order of alto, soprano, tenor and bass and I differ from most people in starting the Fugue not *pianissimo*, but *piano*. The subject of the Fugue is:

The first three voices enter in clear *piano* or *mezzo-piano* tone. At the fifth bar I begin making a *diminuendo* and I bring in the bass voice very quietly, continuing the *diminuendo* down to the end of the sixth bar. Once all four voices have come in it will be seen that at the seventh bar the soprano starts the subject again. If I had begun the Fugue *pianissimo* I should have had to play the new set of voices from the seventh bar much louder, and that bar is so delicately written that the latter would have sounded ugly. I think it is much more interesting to get softer and softer.

The building up of this Fugue must now be considered. Mr. Fuller-Maitland has said that when all the voices are brought in in a different order, the result is called a *Counter Exposition*. From the seventh bar all the voices enter in a different order. In this case the *Counter Exposition* which begins from the seventh bar is very interesting; although Bach keeps on repeating the same theme, by putting it in different 'voices' he makes one feel that the piece is growing and changing. Accordingly I want the student in his playing to build up the Fugue, just as if he were being given masses of new material, instead of the same little phrase repeated again and again. Played thus the Fugue resembles a great architectural tower.

It will be noticed that at the seventh bar, when the *Counter Exposition* begins, the voices, as if impatient, come in sooner than at the beginning, the second voice entering as soon as the first voice has had two quavers. Farther on still, in bars 14 and 15, the four voices make another entry and all are compressed into two bars instead of the six bars they had at the beginning. It is as if the bricks of the tower were getting smaller and smaller towards the top and yet one perceives that the summit is the most important thing about the tower. It is this feeling of building that makes a Fugue so interesting.

From the seventh bar I keep all voices rather quiet until the entrance of the subject in the bass at the seventh bar, where the bass voice goes down to a depth it has not reached before. There is a feeling of pride about it, so that it should be allowed to sound right out and make a firm *crescendo* up to the fourteenth bar. At this point I make the first comma. Having got to *forte* I start off again *piano*, alto voice having the subject. The harmony towards the end of the Fugue gets richer and fuller and the voices come fast one on top of the other, creating a glorious and exhilarating feeling of richness.

### Climax

About the twentieth bar I make a little *diminuendo*, and start off again softly because this zigzag-like bending of the *crescendo* actually makes the eventual climax more emphatic. That climax is reached at bar 24 with the chord of C major. Bars 24 and 25 must be played *forte*, while the last two bars are allowed to die away completely into *pianissimo*.

At the close of this analysis I must again insist upon its personal nature. It is not offered for slavish acceptance, nor is it necessarily my own last word on his music. It is more than likely, indeed, that continued study of this lovely music will show me yet more clearly how Bach meant it to be played.

### PRELUDE AND FUGUE IN C SHARP MINOR

### The Prelude

This Prelude is a very fine study for *legato* playing. Although I use the pedal in the performance of this Prelude, changing it with the main harmonies roughly twice in a bar, the student would do well to practise it without any pedal at all for a while. He should not think of the rhythm as six crotchets in a bar but, curving the line to match the change of pedal, he should think of two long beats in a measure; a slight *porta-*

*mento* accent on the first of the six-quaver groups, anyway for the first four bars, helps in the rhythmic sweep.

The quaver group in bar 4, L.H., should diminish right to the end of the bar, but in the R.H. there should be a *crescendo* towards bar 5 which should be sung out in a good *mezzo-piano* (always keeping the rhythmic curve of two in a bar), then a *diminuendo* at the end of bar 6. The playing should be kept quiet during bars 7 and 8. There should be a *crescendo* in bar 9 to the middle of bar 10, the L.H. coming up a little in bar 11. For bar 12 make it *poco forte*, gradually quietening again for bars 13 and 14. The whole piece is really one long phrase up to bar 14.

It is necessary in part playing when holding long notes with the thumb in the R.H., to use the little finger in the quaver phrases of the upper part where one would otherwise have used the thumb if it were not holding down a long note. In bar 5 the little finger reaches the crotchet 'A' and the fingering should be in the last six quavers of the R.H.— 5 4 3 5; in the next bar, the last six quavers should be fingered —5 4 5; and finally in bar 7 the fingering of the last six quavers should be—5 4 3 2 5. This style of fingering must be considered and used right throughout this piece.

From bar 15 there should be an emotional lull, and I like the playing to be kept very quiet; even when nuances of tone are used, it should all be behind a veil as it were. At the end of bar 17 the *crescendo* in the L.H. last group of six quavers should be *molto*. In the next bar there should be a *crescendo* in the R.H. up to the '♭', with a *diminuendo* on the last six quavers of the bar. These nuances should be imitated in the next bar.

In bar 20 each group of quavers in the L.H. and R.H. should

sing up to F♯ in the L.H. and F♯ in the R.H. and then quiet down in the following bar. The singing tone goes up to D♯ in the L.H. and E in the R.H., bars 23/23 gradual *diminuendo*.

Another similar *crescendo* phrase starts on bars 24/25. The tone is kept up till bar 26 and really goes right on in *crescendo* until bars 27/28, although bar 27 should be started momentarily less only to come up again immediately. In other words, this is a break in the curve and enables one to make the climax *poco forte* instead of using much tone. I always use these zigzags of tone so that there is a feeling of constant building up and *crescendo*, and yet actually in sheer sound one has not increased to a real *forte*; thereby, one has the feeling of great building and tension, saving up the actual climax, as in this case, for bar 32, where the first actual *forte* singing tone should be played and kept up for two bars. A *diminuendo* should occur on bar 34. All these B♯ in the last two bars will have led us to suppose we would close on the C♯ minor chord, but note the subtle tension in the way Bach brings in A♯, L.H., bar 35, thus postponing the close for four more bars. All these last bars should be played in a quiet manner. Great attention should be paid to the 'harmonic' progressions in the part playing, so that this holding up, as it were, of the final 'home' chord which resolves on a familiar *Tierce de Picardie*[1] is shown to be deliberate. Here is a case in point of the emotional necessity behind the composer's innovations that I mentioned in a previous chapter.

*The Fugue*

In this magnificent Fugue of Five Voices, I feel that Bach

[1] See Grove's Dictionary or Enc. Britt.

was preparing himself for such works as the great Triple Fugue, the St. Anne's, for the organ. I always have thought of Fugue No. IV as a Triple Fugue, although I suppose a pedant would say that the second and third parts are really only an extension of, or working out of, the first statement. By thinking of it as a Triple Fugue one can make a more magnificent build-up and get a longer line.

Set the statement of the Fugue at a *grave e sostenuto tempo*. The theme should be *poco forte e sempre marcato* and the feeling should be stern and deep. I make a *diminuendo* on bars 6–7 and 8. The second statement of the Fugue, bar 12, should enter in the R.H. *piano* and *dolce* and the crotchets in the L.H. should be very very quiet. This quietness should be kept up to bars 17, 18 and 19 where for two bars there is a *crescendo*.

The next statement of the Fugue entering in the middle of bar 19, in the L.H., will keep up the tone at which we have arrived; make a *diminuendo* on bar 21. I want a *subito piano* in the R.H. halfway through bar 22.

The theme is next stated in bar 25 where it should be *marcato* (L.H.). In the working out which follows, I would like a *poco crescendo* and a *diminuendo* on bars 31 and 32. The *diminuendo* must continue in bars 33 and 34. There should be no *ritenuto* at this, the end of the first Fugue, as I like to think it.

The next main portion of this great work starts on bar 35. The quavers should be sung out *cantabile, poco mezzo-piano* and this tone should be kept up until halfway through bar 39 and all of bar 40 where it should go right down to *pp*. Meanwhile the first Fugue will be hinted at in a slightly changed rhythm in the L.H. This should not stand out too much as the actual fugal statement comes in the R.H. bar 38 below the lovely weaving of the new melody.

Bar 44 and especially bar 45 are the hardest to play in the whole work. The first theme should be heard again and stated very *marcato* R.H., and the second theme in the L.H. should make a *crescendo* all through bar 45. Care must be taken that the G♯ semibreve in the R.H. is held down with the thumb throughout the bar. In bar 45 the fugal theme goes from B♯, second finger R.H., to the E, fourth finger R.H. Very great care should be taken with the D♯, third finger, second beat, R.H., which should be kept quiet, continuing to its own part, which is C♯, second finger crotchet, always smoothly and quietly so as not to interfere with the fugal theme which is so close to it. All voices at this point should be practised separately and then combined in one hand, and then with the other until all four parts are ready to be played together.

From bar 46 there is a *poco crescendo* leading up to bar 39 where the third of our fugues is introduced, but this *crescendo* must not be heavy at any time. We have the solemn and deep full fugue which is the main fugue. We have the *legato* singing theme in quavers which I call the second, and the third and final fugal entry which must be *marcato* and more lively in performance, albeit as rhythmical as the first one. All three are combined happily at bar 51 and 52 onwards.

I should like the main theme which comes in the L.H. well sung out, but no *forte* at bar 50. This will not cover up the third theme which comes in the next bar, R.H. *mezzo-forte*.

In between these two themes we get the second *cantabile* one, heard *pianissimo*.

The student, for the next few bars, must use his own discretion as to the quality of tone with which the themes will enter and vie and alternate with one another. I myself bring the general tone gradually down to bar 64 where the theme should enter *pianissimo*, getting still quieter for the next bar and a half. The main theme comes in D♯, little finger, R.H. bar 66. This should be very quiet but piercing in quality. Start a big *crescendo* from bar 68. The second theme, quavers in the R.H., should be rather heavily played; the third theme in the L.H. now begins to stand out. Care must be taken in the next few bars (70–4) that the *crescendo* is not overdone and the whole piece must be played up to the *forte* of bar 74, where the main theme comes in, in rather a clanging way in the bass, a *molto marcato*. Exciting though it is, we must remember that the ultimate climax of the piece is not for several more lines, and there must always be a feeling that there is much more to come and we must not force the tone in any way. It is the holding back, through the zigzags of tone that I have described in the Prelude, that gives this tension and mounting climax. The entries of the different fugal themes can be made clear by the skilful tapering off, not too much of course, of the previous theme, just enough to enable the new voice to be heard. We have to remember in this gigantic work that not only are, as is usual in all Fugues, the themes coming in different voices or parts, but three different fugal themes are often introduced and worked out in their varying voices at the same time.

From about bar 85, or even two bars earlier, we begin to quieten and find ourselves on *pp*. in all parts at bar 89, where the first part is stated. In bar 90, the second theme is stated and in bar 92, the third. They are now all working together and though each entry might come *pp*. *p*. to *mezzo-piano*, the whole tenor of the piece is quiet.

From bar 94 the theme should come in *poco mezzo-forte*, in

fact the tone of all the parts should be very rich and vital and increasingly *forte* and always in a singing and noble way. Whilst it is wrong to hurry, there must be a feeling of momentum and the music should keep moving towards the great and final climax, at last set in motion from bar 94.

*N.B.* For very small hands, I keep the pedal on for the whole of bar 97 to enable the semibreve to be held on.

The most wonderful chord in the whole piece surely must be that in bar 109. From bar 105 onwards everything that is noble and sublime should try to come through the fingers and arms, strong but relaxed, in this most magnificent of endings. If there is a *ritardando* made for the last five bars, it must be imperceptible. I leave this to the artist.

# CHAPTER VI

# *Mozart*

For he on honey-dew hath fed,
And drunk the milk of Paradise.
COLERIDGE, *Kubla Khan.*

I remember reading a very interesting article in *Music and Letters* on Mozart by a Frenchman, Arthur Lourié. M. Lourié writes:

'First of all it is necessary to receive and assimilate Mozart, liberating his music from the hard crust of the dead traditionalism and conventionality which have grown around it by this time. In this consists almost the chief difficulty with regard to it, and this it is which makes him really accessible only to a very few in these days.'

In most of the sonatas all the expression marks, i.e. *forte, mezzo-forte, piano,* etc., must be treated as purely relative, the extremes that one uses, namely *pianissimo* and *double-forte,* setting the standard, and the *mezzo-fortes, fortes* and *pianos* being relative to them. It is obvious that these delicate and often rather thin pieces do not require real *forte,* and the indication *piano* should be taken to mean what we know as *pianissimo.*

It is safe to assume that a composer always overmarks his

93

music. Whereas composers are of different nationalities, different temperaments, and therefore require different sorts of tone, such as very big or very small, a thin quality or a thick quality, there is only *one* system of marking. Therefore, it must be remembered that no composer's quality of sound (the lovely French word *timbre*, meaning tone, expresses this) is the same as any other.

Ernest Newman says that people would understand Mozart sonatas so much better if they knew his operas, and that knowledge of the operas would again and again give a clue as to the meaning and performance of certain passages in the sonatas.

I consider Mozart's slow movements the hardest things in music to play. In spite of *pianos* and *fortes*, *phrasing*, *crescendos* and *diminuendos*, *staccato* and *legato*, *accents* and *rests*, *pedalling* and *tone colour*, it should all be as spontaneous and simple as a natural spring gushing forth from the earth. Just as an artist who paints at a foot's distance from the canvas gets in every detail, and yet in his mind's eye sees the picture as a whole, so must the student work at every detail yet remember the whole picture that he has to present. Most people play Mozart *allegros* and *allegrettos* much too quickly, rattling out the semiquavers in a mechanical way and at a speed which no singer or violinist would attempt to use to make sense of similar semiquaver groups in this composer's vocal and orchestral works. To my mind these semiquaver groups have a purely melodic significance and should not be treated as just 'runs'. The student in letting himself go in these colourful and expressive moments must remember to keep everything moving in an unbroken line, and never for one second must he stop listening to the rhythm. It is not enough to feel the rhythm: one must listen to it. All change of tone, colour and quality should be kept within the pulse of the piece and no personal feeling ever be thrust upon the music.

### SONATA IN C MAJOR, K. 330

There was a little Eleventh Pianoforte Sonata of Mozart . . . the playing of this by Harriet Cohen had caught his breath by its sheer loveliness, he had experienced that shuddering sense of perception which was his private signal of the presence of eternal beauty. It was Mozart that he had loved to the point of fearing. At last he had seen through the exterior aristocracy of that music into its inner and most pure of poetry.—RALPH BATES, *Lean Men*.

This sonata is to be begun with a *mezzo-piano* which is sharpened up, so that the resultant brightness will make it sound almost like a *mezzo-forte*. A sort of edge should be given to the tone with the first two G's in bar 1, the rest being *mezzo-piano*. The left hand is *piano* throughout the first four bars. I personally prefer a slow trill in bar 2, thus:

Fifth bar, left hand *pianissimo*. Seventh bar, left hand only, *mezzo-forte* (comparative). In the seventh bar we have the second inversion of the chord of C major, then the dominant seventh of C major going towards the tonic chord of C major in the 8th bar. Therefore, as one plays the 7th bar one should have an imaginary arrow in mind, leading towards the 8th bar, with a *portamento* accent on D♯. The second note in the right hand should be played much softer. The phrase in the left hand, starting with the second semiquaver C, should be *subito piano* after the accent, with a little nuance of tone of the middle of the bar, thus $<\,>$, to show the harmony, tailing off to a *pianissimo* in bar 9, the right hand being just *piano*. Throughout the sonata the accompaniment is just one shade less in tone than the tune. In the 11th bar a *comparative forte* may be used, keeping the tone well up in the next bar. No 'tinkling' effect whatsoever must be permitted in this demi-semiquaver passage and a clear-cut division should be observed between that *forte* and the *piano* in the next bar (13).

The G in bar 18 is the point to which one should be playing, and this note should be not exactly accented, but sung with a pure, clear tone, with a *diminuendo* immediately following, giving the end of the phrase that wistful character which is so very characteristic of Mozart. The left hand in the same bar (18) bursts out in rather a jolly manner, dispelling the faint hint of tragedy that there might otherwise have been. This is the beginning of the secondary subject of the sonata, the first eighteen bars being concerned with the principal subject.

The left hand in this passage must be made to play *semi-staccato, mezzo-forte*, with the *diminuendo* towards the end of the bar—almost in a comic manner, when tears are dispelled in this April music. Bar 19 should be played thus:

bar 19

It is important that the semiquaver rests receive their full value and I think it is better to hold on the G's in the bass as though they were crotchets. If this music were scored for orchestra the probability is that one instrument would hold on the two crotchet G's while another instrument played the semiquaver groups. Also, the D♯ in bar 20 ought to carry a little *portamento* accent, the bass being kept quiet otherwise so that the *mezzo-forte* in the next bar comes as a surprise. I personally do not keep the *mezzo-forte* throughout the bar, but make a *diminuendo* on the triplet, keeping the second half of the bar *piano*, but of course with a little inclination towards the first D in the next bar, taking care to make a *diminuendo* with the next four notes of this bar. This jolly phrase is now repeated, and in the second part of it, bar 24, a *crescendo* should be worked up towards the *forte* in bar 25, the whole passage in this bar being played in a round singing manner. There is an observable difference between bars 20 and 24: bar 20 is *piano* all the time, while in bar 24 a *crescendo* gives a longer line to the music. I prefer the trill in bar 26 played thus:

The second half of bar 32 begins the *codetta*. I always play the *legato* group of semiquavers with a tiny *crescendo* towards the next bar, playing this first note suddenly *pianissimo* and the ensuing notes still softer. I often do this sort of thing at the end of a Mozart phrase, because it gives an enchanting, tender, appealing quality. The *sforzando* on D in bar 34 should be a very small one, otherwise it makes one feel that there is something new coming, when in reality this phrase is only an extra tailpiece, as it were, to the *codetta*. This bar is in the same key and must be played in a rather quieter manner than the preceding bar. The trill in bar 37 would be written out thus:

*bar 37*

The second half of bar 39 and the whole of bar 40 should be played *portamento*, making the *crescendo* go right on to the *forte* of the E in the right hand, bar 41, but dropping the left hand to a *subito pianissimo*.

Bar 42 begins the second *codetta* and good taste demands that the tone of bar 43 be kept up. I dislike passages to be played in the form of echoes. A good *crescendo* in bar 45 is necessary, followed by a drop in tone *subito* on D (bar 46) which needs to be played softly and tenderly. The trill in bar 47 is executed in this way:

*bar 47*

Bars 48 and 49 need playing quietly but without any suspicion of echoes. In bar 51 as a contrast to bar 45 the *crescendo* should be allowed to go straight on to bar 52, the D being

permitted to sing out clearly. The *crescendo* must not be too
hastily dropped in this bar.

## The Middle Section

Before approaching the middle section (after the double
bar) it is necessary to consider that essential difficulty of the
piano which I briefly mentioned in the Introduction. The
bowed and wind instruments alone are able to sustain the full
value of a note, while in the percussion instruments, of which
the piano is one, the note begins to decline in force from the
moment the hammer falls back. It is therefore very important,
when taking a bar like the first bar in the middle section, to
give plenty of tone to the dotted quaver because it is a long
duration, whereas the ensuing notes must be played softer
because they are only semiquavers, i.e. they are short durations.

The first bar of this middle section needs prolonged examination. It is obvious that the semiquavers need a little *crescendo*, that is, a little nuance of tone, to make the phrase go
on towards the next bar. But a soft commencement on the
first dotted quaver, D, will make the semiquavers more important than the dotted quaver. This, as I have explained
above, is against the law of Duration. To put this right I
always sound out the D *mezzo-piano* with a beautiful clear
tone, immediately dropping the tone to start the semiquaver
phrase on the D♯ quite softly. In this way, I think, one can
make a lovely curve of tone (softening at the last semiquaver)
towards the D of the next bar, the left hand being *piano* as
always. The phrasing is to be repeated in the ensuing bars,
each time with a little more tone, so that the *sforzandos* do

not come as too much of a shock. Bar 64 should be persuaded
to sing out boldly.

Here is a case that illustrates Ernest Newman's *operatic*
contention. In the second half bar 66 I make a little *crescendo*
towards the E in bar 67, placing a distinct comma after the D,
which should be played more softly than the E. The next
phrase, starting on C, should be played *pianissimo*, with the
same little nuance towards the next bar as was observed in
the previous bar, but on a very much smaller scale, and with a
*poco ritenuto*. This *ritenuto* will make the pause between the
phrases a shade longer. The next group should start *a tempo*,
*mezzo-piano*, immediately making a *crescendo*, and should
be played in a passionate way. This 'operatic' phrase, as I call
it, seems as if someone had nearly given in about something
and then at the last moment made a violent protest and said:
No! I won't! From the *crescendo* bars 69 and 70 must sing out
all the way to the F quaver, the G in the left hand being held
as long as possible during the *crescendo* bar, because it gives a
harmonic background to the phrase. At the end of bar 70 a
very big *diminuendo* in the last two notes in the left hand is
essential, a lesser *diminuendo* in the right hand accompanying
it. The C in the next bar must sing *mezzo-piano*. The left hand
should be very quiet by now.

This bar 71 begins the intermediate subject of this section.
After the sung-out C in bar 71 I proceed quietly, making the
phrase go towards A of bar 75. In other words, make a very
slight *crescendo* from C through B♭. The trill itself must be
played very softly as must the grace note group in bar 71:

It is a good idea to hold on the first note of each semiquaver group in the left hand to help show the changes in harmony.

After the sung-out A in bar 73, it is well to play the next note, C, more *piano*, then *crescendo*, singing out in a most ardent manner towards the A in the next bar, making a *diminuendo* towards the second half of the bar. In bar 75, a *diminuendo* towards the second half of the bar is advisable, likewise in the following bar, which should start *pianissimo* and get still softer towards the end of the bar. Bar 78:

Care is needed in bar 79 and the following bars to observe the semiquaver rests in the right hand. These little breaths add to the poignancy of this exquisite phrase. The left hand in these bars, 79 to 82, should be played *portamento*, e.g. bar 79:

I play the grace notes in bar 83 in triplet demisemiquaver groups. Bar 84 is best given *mezzo-forte* but the demisemiquaver groups in bar 85 require *mezzo-piano* leading to *crescendo*, which brings us back to the principal subject in bar 88.

From bar 88 onwards is a repetition of the first section and should be played in the manner I have already described. Bar 129, I personally play like this:

You can use this version or:

The last few bars again require careful attention; one notices that in this repetition, bar 140 is identical with bar 134. Where this same bar occurs in the first section (47) its repetition in that section (53) is slightly different. This is only a little thing but I like to get all details perfect. The smallest thing in art is worthy of the greatest patience and service.

This *codetta* is a little more elaborated than the first one. I am sure Mozart, once he had created that poignant and divinely beautiful middle section, could never have felt quite the same again as he went on to construct this first movement.

The principle of tone values that I suggested for the middle section should also be adopted here. In the left hand I make the *crescendo* in the upper part go right up to the B♭ (bar 146) followed by an immediate reduction, the tone of the right hand being reduced a shade earlier, just before the semiquaver F. A gradual *diminuendo* towards the end of the piece now becomes necessary.

## THE SLOW MOVEMENT

### The First Section

The first few notes of this movement must sing out in a clear calm manner. It ought to be remembered that the phrase is going to the G in bar 2; therefore in the playing of the first three quaver C's too much emphasis must not be directed on playing towards the C in bar 1, while the left hand must be kept quiet all the time. In the second half of bar 2 I use only a *mezzo-forte*, the left hand being *mezzo-piano*, dropping to *piano* on the first inversion of the B♭ chord in bar 3; and I am always careful not to play the demisemiquavers too quickly and to keep the phrase going towards the fourth bar. The end of the phrase should be quite *piano*, with a little nuance of tone towards the second inversion of the chord of F major, especially towards the right hand A. The turn is to be played thus:

The *sforzando* in bar 5 is only a little one and one should be careful not to overdo it. In the second *sforzando* a little more tone can be given to the left hand to bring out the harmony, making an immediate *diminuendo* on the second beat. Let this phrase progress towards the second beat in bar 7 (inversion of the chord of C major), nevertheless the curve of the phrase may be shown by a little *portamento* weight on the semiquaver C♯. After the C♯ a *diminuendo* towards the next bar gives point.

The phrase beginning after the double bar is another of those operatic phrases; I play the semiquavers with a suspicion of a break between each two, thus:

and I find that the phrase thus conveys a suggestion of opera. For the same reason one should separate the last chord in bar 9 in this way making the accent on the next bar clearer, repeating this at the end of the next bar. No *crescendo* is needed in bar 11; the tone should be kept very soft with only a shade of a delicate curve at the half-bar, and the little groups slightly separated, though with hardly anything so definite as a slur. The whole phrase is going towards bar 12. The grace note group in bar 11 may be played as four semiquavers. The quaver C's must not be commenced too softly though one should be careful in the *forte* chord not to hit the keys. The pianist should think of this chord being played with a bow on strings. The E♮'s in bar 14 must sing out, and the E♭ of bar 15; the rest of the notes of the trill being quite soft, with the left hand very quiet.

The *sforzando* in bar 16 should be very minute, the crotchet rest in the left hand being very important and it gives a pathetic quality to the phrase. Bar 17 begins another operatic phrase, and a bold *crescendo* is desirable here, the left hand giving good support to the upper part in bar 18. Care must be taken not to make the demisemiquaver C's too small, which would take away the essential operatic personality of the phrase. The next four graceful semiquavers should go towards the inversion of the F major chord on the second beat, with a *diminuendo* towards the next bar.

### The Middle Section

The next section always reminds me of Schubert, and I think that he must have particularly loved this movement, and that he owed more to Mozart than many people realize.

The whole section must be played very softly, being thought of as containing one beat in a bar. The bottom F may be held for one quaver so that it conveys the effect of a little slur; there should be no attempt, however, to make any of the other F's *legato*. The passage must be pedalled thus:

I cannot sufficiently emphasize the necessity for playing this section with the utmost simplicity. I would rather have too little colour than too much. The word expression would be best forgotten while playing this section.

The *acciaccaturas* in bars 24 and 25 are played *on* the beat and the ornament in bar 26 thus:

bar 26

A very soft commencement must be given to the phrase after the double, *mezzo-forte* is quite enough even in bar 30. In bar 31, the C is marked *sforzando*. In the following bar there is no real need to emphasize the C, the strange-sounding D♮ and the ensuing notes will do that satisfactorily, in the same way that in painting, the dark shadows intensify the light. The most important thing in all this, I feel, is to keep the one-in-a-bar feeling. For the rest, the only necessary detail is to play the top part in the R.H. in bar 35 as four semiquavers and to give the whole movement the quality of a duet for violin and 'cello, with occasional parts for the whole orchestra.

### The Last Section

The first subject now returns. From bar 60 onwards is a *codetta*—an elaboration in the major key of our middle subject. It is as though Mozart wanted to remind us of the rather sad middle subject, although he gives it here in a happier mood. There is an opening expanding character in the music so that the tone must be kept up until the third beat of bar 62. Here a sudden drop in the left hand is demanded by the feeling of the music.

In this *codetta* I use the pedal for the third beat of each bar only.

### THE THIRD MOVEMENT

I am not going to say a great deal about this movement: the student will now be able to work out his interpretation with the aid of my comments on the previous two movements. It should be noted that the *tempo* is *allegretto* and the temptation to play too quickly should be resisted.

The movement must be begun in a quiet, rather demure fashion. Although bar 9 is marked *forte*, it must not be given too vigorous a handling, *mezzo-forte* in the L.H. is quite loud enough. All grace notes, turns and trills are to be executed in the same way as in the preceding movements, the trill in bar 4 thus:

The singing tone must be maintained in the R.H. in bar 13, giving to the L.H. a lighter tone.

The triplets in bars 16, 17, 18 and 19 need *piano* presentation: by this means a *mezzo-forte* effect will be obtained as there are more notes in each bar, which if they were played *mezzo-forte* would actually sound *forte* in tone. Throughout this passage the arm must be lightly poised over the keyboard and the body must be held so that it is quite free in its movements from side to side.

The first note in bar 21 should be allowed to sing out clearly, while the ensuing notes must be performed in a rather nonchalant manner, so achieving a slight change of mood. The grace notes in this bar have the value of demisemiquavers. The R.H. in the last half of bar 22 and the first half of bar 23 is marked *staccato*, but I personally prefer *portamento*, making a curve of tone towards bar 24, followed by an immediate *diminuendo* on the demisemiquavers. The L.H. should be played very quietly and smoothly in these four bars, with a little more tone in bar 25, the tone being kept up throughout the bar, making a *diminuendo* on the first beat of the next bar. If one makes an ordinary *crescendo* from the second beat of bar 26, through bar 27, bar 28 is apt to sound too loudly. An amusing way of getting a *crescendo* and yet confining it to narrow tone limits is to begin *staccato*, then play *semi-staccato* and finish up *portamento*. In this case the first four semiquavers would be *staccato*, the next four less *staccato* and the last four *portamento*, which, while achieving an apparent *crescendo*, enables one to arrive at bar 28 playing only *mezzo-forte*, the exact volume of tone required.

In the next few bars my former remarks about the triplet bars should be borne in mind. The third bar of this phrase (bar 31) make a *diminuendo* and the *crescendo* in the L.H. in bar 32 should not be very big, while the left hand in bars 32, 34, 35 and 36 must be kept very quiet. No *crescendo* in bar 35 is desirable, but a little nuance of tone will lead the music towards bar 37. In this latter bar I play the grace note G with the L.H. B. The trills in bars 39, etc., all receive this value:

bar 39

and should be played very softly. There must be considerable variation in volume hereabouts, a *crescendo* in the second half of bar 41 must be followed by a *diminuendo* in bar 42, leading to the C in bar 43. A *crescendo* in bar 45 leads to a *mezzo-forte* in bar 46. This triplet passage should be played rather fussily, in a rather comic fashion, but not too loudly, and it should be thought of as four quavers in a bar rather than two crotchets.

In bars 49 and 50 I make a slight *crescendo* towards the dominant chord in bar 51, in bars 50, 52, etc., taking care to hold the crotchet in the L.H. for its full value. The greatest precision in *duration* helps the phrasing. The grace notes in bars 60 and 62 should be played as triplets.

### The Middle Section

Here is the operatic mood again. The first four bars should be played in a rather sulky, bad-tempered way, but barely *mezzo-piano* in volume. A somewhat square treatment suits the music perfectly, the L.H. as loud as the R.H., especially in bars 70 and 71. In bar 72, the mood changes completely, the imaginary recalcitrant of the first four bars is immediately sorry for his outburst and these next few bars should be played in the most tender, charming manner, with a little *diminuendo* from the first quaver to the second so that the first has a singing and appealing quality. The trill:

should be as light as feathers. The *sforzando* in bar 73 should be of the slightest, with immense care in the pedalling of this passage, so that the semiquaver rests are quite apparent.

After this April display the music starts off with a long wistful phrase, during which the R.H. should be very quiet and the L.H. *pianissimo*. A tiny *crescendo* is pleasant in bar 78 towards the *fp* in bar 79. Bars 78 to 83 consist of two-bar phrases. The first must be given very softly, the second should be given a little more tone, the third a little more tone still, so that each two-bar phrase grows out of the previous one. A not too vigorous singing tone is desirable for this section. Then a tiny *crescendo* in bar 90 to bar 91 subsides at once to a *pianissimo*, leading back to the repetition of the first subject. In this section (from bar 78) it is well to hold on the first semiquaver of each semiquaver group so that it sounds like a crotchet, as described to you in the first movement.

I play the last section in the manner described for the first. Bar 123 is marked *forte*, but I find it undesirable to force the tone of this passage, bearing in mind all that was said about rotary freedom. In bars 125 and 126 I prefer the following fingering: for the last three semiquavers in 125 I use 4 3 1, in bar 126 I use 2, then 1 2 4 2 1, then in the normal way.

The last few bars of the movement should be performed in a light, dancing manner. In this section the R.H. contains three notes to every two of the L.H. and some difficulty may therefore be experienced in getting it to play correctly with its partner. If this is so, on no account should the practice of trying to make the hands fit be indulged in.

# CHAPTER VII

# *Chopin*

Elle avait appris dans sa jeunesse à caresser les phrases, au long col sinueux et démesuré, de Chopin, si libres, si flexibles, si tactiles, qui commencent par chercher et essayer leur place en dehors et bien loin de la direction de leur départ, bien loin du point où on avait pu espérer qu'atteindrait leur attouchement, et qui ne se jouent dans cet écart de fantaisie que pour revenir plus délibérément, d'un retour plus prémédité, avec plus de précision, comme sur un cristal qui résonnerait jusqu'à faire crier, vous frapper au coeur.— MARCEL PROUST.

Many people have the idea that the secret of playing Chopin's music lies in the use of *rubato*, in allowing oneself great liberties with the *tempo*. My opinion is that it should be played *as much in time as possible*, and that we are not entitled to alter phrases so much that they are scarcely recognizable.

In Guy de Pourtalès's *Life of Chopin* we are told that Chopin became very angry when people accused him of permitting too much freedom with *tempo*. 'Your left hand should be the "choirmaster" whilst your right hand should be allowed to play *ad libitum*', he said. And from what we know of Chopin's own musical preferences and in particular of his manner of preparing for a concert it is impossible to believe that one of such stringent taste could have been so lax and unmusical, for that is what it amounts to, as certain performers would have us believe. Chopin did not want the elasticity of any right-hand passages which might need a certain amount of freedom to interfere with the rigid *tempo* of the piece as a whole. The left hand must keep the *tempo* even, while the right hand supplies any variations in speed.

Mr. William Murdoch in his biography of Chopin said that Chopin 'often surprised and delighted his pupils by playing them short recital programmes after their lessons. Bach was usually chosen for this purpose. Not only did he worship the "48" but he was anxious that his pupils should share his appreciation.' Again it is difficult to believe that the following could be true of a man so libertine in *tempo* as one tradition wishes us to believe. 'Chopin preferred Mozart's music to all others, especially *Don Giovanni*, whilst for Bach he had the greatest reverence; he always prepared for his concerts by playing the Preludes and Fugues.'

### ETUDE IN C SHARP MINOR OP. 27, NO. 5

Chopin was a very nervous, highly strung, sensitive being, and the student must feel his music in that way; then, when he plays his music, that inner feeling will come through into the finger-tips and communicate itself to the very key and string which is used.

### *The Introduction*

A sensitive, almost hesitating or timid manner of playing is demanded by the *lento* introduction. It is absolutely pre-ludial in character, vagrant and unsettled, and so it may be played quite freely as regards time, provided that the phrase is not broken up in any way and its general shape not distorted, for that would be to rob it of its perfection as a prelude.

One of the difficulties in this Etude is to keep the quaver accompaniment in the R.H. absolutely steady, quiet and even. The fingers must be allowed to rest on the surface of the keys, for in order to get an absolute *legato* on repeated notes such as these the keys must not come right up to the top, but must be depressed sufficiently to produce the sound required, just before they do this. It is vitally important that the time and tone of this accompaniment throughout be absolutely even. The accompaniment holds together the two songs, sometimes heard as a duetto and sometimes as a solo—soprano and alto they may be considered.

*Example 1*

The first twenty bars should be played with great feeling, but with restraint also, because on the third page the original theme returns and must then be played in an even more intense manner. The tone of both alto and soprano songs must have a *living* quality.

In bar 6 it will be seen that there are three quavers to a beat in the left hand and two to a beat in the right hand. There must be no indulgence in the futile practice of trying to 'fit' the two parts together, the rhythms of each must be mentally appropriated by practising each hand separately. During final performance attention to these independent rhythms will achieve the necessary fusion into a musical whole. For the trill in bar 7, example 1 will probably be found sufficient.

A sudden *pianissimo* in the accompaniment in bar 9 will allow the L.H. melody to sing out in the way it should; while in bar 10, the R.H. melody must be heard prominently also, but a little more softly. In bar 11, the new harmony calls for a complete drop in tone, the accompaniment in the L.H. being kept very *pianissimo*. A crescendo follows to bar 13. From the second beat of this bar (the dominant of F minor), continuing through the next four bars, everything should be played in the softest possible manner. Chopin's 'choirmaster' here is in the right hand, and the left hand should be played *ad libitum*.

Bar 21 begins a new section of the music, which should be played in a far more agitated manner, though the L.H. passage in bar 22 must not be rushed—a crescendo will make all the excitement necessary; this whole passage must be played strictly in time, too. I use the fingering given in the example reproduced on the next page.

The next two bars are an imitation of bars 21 and 22, only more strident. The song has now become an alto solo. The whole section must continue to move onwards, the *tempo* perhaps a shade faster than the *duetto* of the first section. The trill in bar 25 on B and C♯ is to be performed with as many repetitions as can be managed comfortably, and it must lead *without any turn* straight into bar 26.

If any difficulty is experienced in bar 27 in playing each hand in a separate *tempo* as is indicated, I advise that whilst learning it, and practising it slowly, little time places be made in the left hand to fit in with the right hand chords, so:

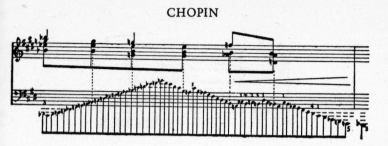

This is how I practised the passage before I was able to play the left-hand part in a straight mad swirl.

### Calm Third Section

The music becomes calmer from bar 28 to the pause, like the sea after a storm; but, although this passage should be played in the calmest possible manner, there still remains in the L.H. an undercurrent of the tragic upheaval of the previous bars.

I play from the pause to bar 38 in an absolutely 'dead' manner; the music is too worn out for any more feeling. The passage must be performed in time, without any feeling at all, with care to play both hands exactly together. The music must fade away completely, like the last flicker of a candle flame, on this chord:

The trill in bar 37 should have this value:

The alto voice now begins to recover, and gradually leads back to the original theme. I play this in a much more intense manner than the first time—without restraint, but taking care that the tone is never hard, and with a sort of *vibrato* quality such as Kreisler often gets with his violin. Although the pianist cannot move his fingers to secure a *vibrato* as a violinist can, it must not be forgotten that the piano string *is* vibrating and the intensity of feeling which is communicated through the fingers by way of the key to the string will cause it to vibrate.

In the chromatic passage in the left hand, bar 52, it is important to use the fourth finger for the two F♯'s and for the C♯ just before the E of the melody. The trill in bar 51 is the same as that in bar 7.

### Final Section

I play the trill in bar 55 with the grace notes before the beat, thus:

The first chord in bar 63 must not be played *arpeggio* unless it is beyond the student's capacity of stretch.

The last fifteen or sixteen bars are full of deep sorrow. Chopin was a very sick man when he wrote this Etude, and his ill health must have affected his mind as well as his body. There must therefore be a measure of sympathy in the pianist's approach to his music, for that is the only thing that can help him to play it as the composer meant it to be played.

### NOCTURNE IN F MAJOR

> Toi qui, comme un coup de couteau,
> Dans mon coeur plaintif est entrée.
> BAUDELAIRE, *Les Fleurs du Mal.*

I have chosen this Nocturne because it is to my mind by far the most beautiful, the most sincere and characteristic of all Chopin's Nocturnes.

Chopin was influenced by the Irish composer John Field, who lived from 1782 to 1837. He studied Field's works very closely and used them as models for his Nocturnes. Field wrote very simple harmonies and elaborated his melodies by embroidering them with fanciful runs and turns. It is very interesting to learn that on Chopin's first public appearance as a performer he played a concerto by this composer.

In this Nocturne Chopin already seems to have got away from his immature style which followed closely that of Field, and which perhaps provides one of the reasons why Chopin's music has often been called drawing-room music. In this Nocturne he has already become much more personal and to me, at any rate, this work expresses the passionate, virile, masculine Chopin of the great works, such as the B Flat Minor Sonata, the Barcarolle, etc.

The first person I ever heard play this piece was Paderewski, and the principal thing in that performance was the almost painful beauty of his singing tone in the R.H. melody—that tone which stabbed one to the heart. The student must aim at this distinction also; his tone here should be sensitive and nervous, and although never hard should have a piercing quality.

In this respect I can only repeat what I have written in the lesson on the Chopin Etude, that quality of tone must come from within the pianist.

### The L.H. Triplets

The double time signature 3/4, 9/8 must not be allowed to cause perplexity. The Nocturne is obviously in 3/4 time, the inside accompaniment of the L.H. being really in triplets. It would have been confusing, however, to write a three over every triplet for a whole page, and Chopin has therefore chosen this manner of conveying his intention. The 9/8 just applies to the inside part of the L.H.

I think it is easier to finger the first chords 5 4 1, using the 4 on the A. It must be remembered that, as in the first chord of this Nocturne (L.H.) whether one is playing chords or single notes, both sides of the hand should always be perfectly free at once. The notes of the L.H. chord in this Nocturne are some way apart from each other, and there will not be room to use much rotary movement in the triplets. It is nevertheless always necessary to be conscious of a slight rotary *exertion* from the A to the C.

The L.H. should be made to play as *legato* as possible before the pedal is used. The minims in the lower part must certainly be sustained, but the crotchet chord must be held on as long as possible, and if possible until that moment when, with a sliding movement of the thumb, the pianist can reach the next crotchet chord. If this is impossible, the crotchet must be held down at any rate until the first C (second quaver) is well over.

*Pedalling*

The student must try to solve the problems of pedalling for himself. It need not be changed much in the first three bars, but with the fourth bar it must be changed at every beat.

This lovely first phrase must sing out with the tone I have described above, with a *diminuendo* in the L.H. on the second and third beats of the fourth bar, as opposed to the *crescendo* marked in some editions. This will enable the A in the R.H. to continue to sound audibly and also it enables the G of the next bar to be sung out in a most poignant manner. The next beat must be dropped to a *subito pp*, which will enable the modern and almost painful harmony of the chord to stand out by contrast. A still further *crescendo* would not only have broken the line of the phrase, but the very volume of sound would have taken the intensity from this 'painful' chord. In bar 5, the student should not try to play two against three, but hold on to R.H. A as long as he can, and play the semi-quaver as late as he dare. From the *subito pianissimo* a gradual and slight *crescendo* will lead towards the seventh bar, the last beat of which must decline with a *diminuendo* towards the end of the phrase in the eighth bar. A change of pedal with the lower note on bar 8 on the E must be carefully made.

Although the second phrase finishes on bar 8, the whole piece must be kept moving right up to the ninth bar, where the theme starts again. The common fault of allowing changes of tone colour, nuance and expression to hinder the proper flow of the music must be watchfully guarded against. In this case the L.H. triplets should be an ever-recurring throb. It is not enough to play this music strictly in time, it must move, flow onwards, almost as if the piece had no bar lines. It is good to bear in mind that excessive *rubatos* and bad sense of line are much harder to hide in a steady regular rhythm such as this in the L.H. than in a piece where the accompaniment is more broken up and varied.

In bar 9, the student must be very careful in the third beat that the pedal comes off with G in the R.H., for the quaver rest is the most important thing in the bar. In the first beat of the next bar, the pedal must come up with the second semi-quaver, while an infinitesimally small accent should fall on the first note of the triplet. I think this demands a rather more subdued manner than the first line, otherwise it should be played the same. However, in the *crescendo* towards the twelfth bar the singing tone must not be quite so strong, because this phrase should merge into the next one, and the Bb R.H. in bar 13 is obviously a higher point. To prevent this excessive tone in the thirteenth bar, the *crescendo* should be made towards bar 15 in the L.H., thus bringing into prominence the beautiful modulating harmonies of the 14th bar. The L.H. top part has become another melodic voice. It will be seen, in fact, that the G of the last bar in the L.H. is carried over to the *acciaccatura* A in the R.H., bar 15.

That must be the reason for Chopin's making the A an *acciaccatura*: this should be played at the same time as the L.H. C. The F and the E in this bar should sing out clearly, with no *piano* as given in some editions. In bar 16 a *diminuendo* is secured especially on the last beat, when bar 17 must sing out again. All nuance and phrasing demands the utmost care, for this first page is divided into phrases of four bars, four bars, eight bars, five bars and finally three bars. A very big *diminuendo* is necessary in the L.H. from bar 17, but only a small-scale one in the R.H., because there the singing tone must be maintained until bar 20. An extreme *diminuendo* in the L.H. will make it seem as if the whole thing were getting softer. The first real drop in the R.H. is on the second beat of bar 20. The first beat of bar 18 should be played thus:

In bar 19 the R.H. sings out alone, the L.H. being *pianissimo*. On the second beat of the L.H. prominence must be given to the L.H. chord so that it can again make a big *diminuendo* to the F major chord on the next beat, and so that the right hand does not have to come down until the *subito* chord above described. In bar 20, the grace notes must be played absolutely evenly, and the speed must not be held up in the slightest degree, for the phrase goes on to the F in bar 22. The grace notes fall like this:

and in this last phrase the instructions in the copy should be carried out, making a *diminuendo* and *rallentando*. Care must be taken to notice that in the L.H. the quaver triplets have been turned into two quavers, bar 24, which of course make it still slower. The word *smorzando*, of course, means extinguished.

### The Con Fuoco Section

This Nocturne could be described, apart from its musical value, as an exercise in rotary freedom. As I have said previously on the subject of the L.H. chords, the pianist's hand should always be perfectly free from both sides at once, whether he is playing notes or chords together or singly. In this *con fuoco* passage what I shall call a combined rotary freedom will be needed.

Apart from the principal accents on the first of each group of six semiquavers, it is wise to give a similar accent on the last quaver beat, that is the last semiquaver but one. We are playing in 9/8 time, which equals three dotted crotchets, and it is a good plan, therefore, when the quaver which equals the dot is reached, to give an accent. I refuse to acknowledge the technical difficulty, because I think it is all bound up with the rhythmical one and, until the rhythm of this piece is under control, quite a big accent can be given on the quaver beat, leading to a still bigger one on the next crotchet beat (first note of the group). In the L.H., first bar, an accent should fall on every note in the first semiquaver group, continuing the accent on 1, 3. 1, until the next beat which is played as usual, i.e. without accenting every note. This makes it sound more ferocious and emphatic. However many technical difficulties are experienced, the musical meaning of this page must be kept constantly in mind. To my mind the L.H. here is not a mere *run* but is like a livid streak of lightning across the sky.

Try to get an enormous amount of tone in this passage by alternating a system of relaxation and exertion, so quick that it is almost impossible to detect where one begins and the other ends.

*Pfz* in bar 29 means *poco sforzando* and not, as might appear, *piano* and then *sforzando*. It means that one must give a little bite of tone into the C. In this bar it will be easier to keep the thumb on the C, L.H., not change it to two. This makes it possible to hold on the minim in the lower part, and slide the thumb on to the D. The accents in the R.H. on the crotchet and quaver beats must not be forgotten, so that the semiquaver chords will fall into their right time places and the difficulties of these bars will disappear. No notice should be taken of the accents in the R.H. in bar 30 given in any edition. The harmony will speak for itself.

In bar 31 the melody is taken over by the R.H. The easy way of fingering bar 31 is: 5th on G♭, 2nd on minim, thumb on F. The 5th finger should be released, the pedal being used to hold down the G♭, and the 2nd finger changed to the 5th. The thumb should be held down on F all the time, which leaves the 3rd finger free to play G♭, and the minim will be held down with the 5th finger for the next bar.

The R.H. must be dropped down to a *piano*, the L.H. starting with a *mezzo-piano*, making an immediate *crescendo* up towards *forte*. Bar 33 should be played *piano* but without a *ritenuto* which would break the momentum of the piece. An echo of the preceding two bars will suffice. In bar 35, the dominant chord must sing out *mezzo-forte*, the R.H. passage starting in 6ths, on the 3rd beat of the bar, *piano* making a *crescendo*. A *ritenuto* may be made towards bar 37. In the 6th passage I will leave the pianist to arrange the fingering most suitable to his own sized hands. Bars 44 and 45 should be *sempre pedale*. I personally hold the pedal down for the whole bar. In bar 43 the R.H. must be kept *piano*, but the L.H. started *mezzo-forte*. In bar 46, an infinitesimal *rallentando* is commenced which will continue towards the Tempo I.

### Return of the First Section

This recapitulation of the first theme should be played in all ways as I have described above, with the sole difference that for the first two or three bars the pianist will steal in *pianissimo* with a very thin note. By about bars 53, 54, 55, the normal tone of the first part must be regained. In bar 56 there is a slight variation of the original bar. If possible it is better to do without the *ritenuto* at the end of bar 55 (and similarly in bar 7) as these bars must lead straight on to the reiteration of the tune in bar 57 (and in bar 9).

In bars 71, 72, the R.H. melody may be supported by giving it the slightest shadow of an accent on the same notes which occur an octave below in the L.H. The spread chords in bars 73, 74, must be played very softly and evenly, care being taken to change the pedal on the first note of each bar.

# CHAPTER VIII

# *Brahms*

Where are the songs of Spring? Ay, where are they?
Think not of them, thou hast thy music too.
KEATS, *Ode to Autumn.*

## INTERMEZZO. OP. 117, NO. 3

This is one of the most characteristic and typical of Brahms's pianoforte pieces, and I am always amazed that it so rarely appears on concert programmes. When I say that I consider it characteristic, I mean that, besides the glowing beauty which Brahms's work possesses, it has also an intellectual depth of the kind often described as the *dark* quality of Brahms's music.

This piece should be begun very softly indeed, nevertheless a very simple device will show the beauty of the phrase in a singularly beautiful way. If for the first two bars the R.H. is kept even softer than the L.H. and then at the third bar it is brought up to the same tonal level, it will be found that this has the effect of presenting the wild, glowing quality of the phrase, with the barest increase of the actual volume of tone.

Pedalling, also, is very important in beginning this Intermezzo. If the pedal is changed at every quaver it will enable the student to preserve the phrasing marked in the original edition. It must be remembered, however, that while the pianist will be pedalling four times in a bar, the phrasing is distinctly towards each crotchet beat. That is to say, it is necessary to think 'two in a bar'.

In bar 6 I keep the L.H. very soft, singing out very slightly the top part in the R.H. So played, this passage should be very charming and plaintive, especially if the R.H. has been played with the right softness in the previous phrase.

In bar 11, both hands must play with equal tone, singing out rather more than the preceding phrases, and this should be continued until the first chord of bar 15, where an immediate *diminuendo* must be heard. In bar 13 the remarks made upon Durations in the Mozart lesson must be borne in mind, the semiquavers being played lighter than the quavers. Bar 11 is the climax of this phrase, and already in bar 16 the tone must begin to drop. A slight *portamento* accent on the first chord of each beat will make the little *diminuendos* in the L.H. effective.

As I have continually emphasized, this care for details must not prevent the pianist from keeping the whole music of this page moving. A slight fault in this direction can be put right at bar 21, when the appearance of the lovely little tune in another disguise will enable the time to be picked up. This is the best fingering for the tune:

The music should be played in a frightened, almost plead-ing manner. It will be noticed that in the next two lines the treatment of the theme becomes more restless. The beauty of the music will be made more apparent if one keeps the top part (consisting of A and C♯), and the L.H. as soft as possible, so that the melody, in the lower part of the R.H., sings steadily. In bars 23, 24, 25, the melody notes come between the two notes of the accompanying chord: the E and C♯ must therefore receive especial care and must be sounded as softly as possible, while the melody is made to sing out more and more. It is a fascinating exercise, this playing of a tune *cantabile*, with a soft accompanying note on either side of it. One must be sure to play all these three notes *dead* together; and in bar 24 to play the L.H. as smoothly as possible. As this bar is likely to cause some difficulty, I propose to explain the way in which I play *legato* octaves. It will certainly help students who cannot stretch the interval of a tenth which Brahms has written.

There must be no dependence on the pedal in the playing of *legato* octaves. In the first place, the actual octave keys must be held depressed as long as possible. Movement is accomplished in this way. When the L.H. is moving upwards, the little finger must be kept upon the key while the thumb is raised and moved forward to the next note, allowing the little finger to reach its note by a *sliding* movement over the surface of the key. When the L.H. is moving downwards, the proceeding is reversed, the little finger being raised to find its next note and the thumb sliding over the key to its appropriate position. The student will easily adapt the procedure to the R.H. and then it will be seen that, in playing *legato* octaves in this manner, one slides over the keys with the thumb or little finger in the rear of the movement, to borrow a term from strategy. I strongly advise the practising of the *arpeggio* of C major in this way also. This would be particularly helpful in facilitating the playing of this bar 24 of Brahms's Intermezzo. Applying the method, the student will first raise the thumb and slide with the little finger, then moving downwards again, he will lift the little finger and slide the thumb. It will be seen that the method can be applied quite well to single notes as well as to octaves played simultaneously. In fact, so applicable is this method of *legato* playing that one might say that the most important general direction for this piece is to insist upon the fingers being kept on the surface of the keys. The fingers *must not leave* the keyboard.

The lower part of the R.H. in the second half of this phrase must continue to sing out, but the music of course becomes more passionate. The phrasing given should be followed. In bars 27 and 28 the 'sliding' method will be needed more than ever in the L.H. and the *crescendo* and *diminuendo* marks must be followed. In bar 27, if it is found that pedalling twice in a bar makes a slightly blurred effect, every quaver may be pedalled.

The next phrase, beginning at the end of bar 30, is played *pianissimo*, as marked, and it must be remembered that all the fingers in both hands are to be played with the same amount of weight. My remarks about the playing of this phrase when it first appeared also apply here, the only difference being that it must be played *pianissimo*, and very *legatissimo*.

The *ritenuto* in the second half of bar 39 should be noticed and a *portamento* accent made on the first note of the next bar.

## The Poco Piu Lento

The *poco piu lento* is sung out a little more. After the extreme quiet of the preceding bars this lovely coda comes as a cry from the heart, and should be played in a most plaintive way. The *diminuendos* Brahms has marked do not apply to the L.H., but are a reminder to play the semiquavers lighter than the dotted crotchets. In other words, the Durations must be remembered. This *lento* should be played most expressively and should be thought of as one in a bar.


## A New Section

In the next part, beginning in bar 45, Brahms means the music to move on in time, and although it is to be played softly it must be played expressively. The depth and gloom of the preceding part have lightened, and this part should be played very gracefully. The phrases should be exquisitely rounded, and the player should lean most tenderly and caressingly on the syncopated melody notes (semiquaver tied to a dotted quaver), keeping the semiquaver accompaniment in both hands very quiet. The whole section is on a very small scale.

The phrase must lead to the minim C in the R.H., with a warm tone on the first note of bar 45 (tied from the previous semiquaver). The A in the bass should be warmly played, but immediately afterwards the L.H. passage is started very softly, a curve of tone being made as indicated by the composer. In this L.H. semiquaver passage, bar 49, Tobias Matthay's rule of rotary movement should be observed, i.e. the pianist must rotate in the direction of the next finger, not of the next note. The hand should roll well over to the right, with the thumb on the A, and although the next note is to the right of the one just played, the next finger which will be used is on the left of the thumb; therefore the pianist must rotate in the direction of the thumb. This semiquaver passage is fingered thus: 5214, 3212, 3413, 421. This phrase must be played so that it is shown distinctly as a four-bar phrase. These first four bars must be kept very quiet, otherwise there will be nothing left to do in the next four bars, which must also be on the soft side.

The repetition of the phrase beginning in bar 50 should be treated in exactly the same way as before. The C♯ in bar 52 must sing out, for this is the first indication of the very lovely modulation to the key of E major, and the composer's expression marks should be followed.

In bar 53 the key of E major has already been reached, therefore the last bars of this phrase should be played with less tone, although it must be clearly indicated that the phrase goes to the last bar. The repeat should not be omitted.

The pianist will probably find that in this next page, from bar 56 onwards, his tone will insensibly increase a little and this is all to the good. As this part is obviously more agitated a more intense singing tone on the tied melody notes can be substituted for the caressing tone used previously for the melody.

Nevertheless up to the *forte* in bar 59 the semiquavers should be kept quiet as before, not omitting to show the descent of the bass from the E♯ at the double bar to the D in the *forte* bar.

In bar 61, the phrase is started very softly and the harmony does not change as in the previous part. Therefore, the change of bass note from the third to the seventh note of the dominant chord must be shown. The pianist must not be afraid of getting too much tone in these bars, as they are the climax of this page. It will be noticed that the bass note here is E instead of the A which begins this section, so that the beginning of the phrase is not definitely arrived at again until bar 66.

It will be noticed that in bar 70 the L.H. is slightly changed and this phrase should therefore be played in a rather more tentative way than on its first appearance, as if it were not quite sure whether it was going back to the E major or not. Here again I advise the student to repeat the whole page as indicated.

The pause marked at the end of this section must be very carefully observed and the pedal lifted before beginning the next exquisite phrase which leads back to the original theme in bar 81. This phrase (bar 76 to 81) must be played *pianissimo* as marked, and as *legato* as possible. I use this fingering for the little quaver groups, taking care to slide down with the fifth finger:

5

4    5

12    4

12

It has been remarked that an actor's words were like honey in his mouth and one should be able to say here that the notes were like honey in the pianist's hands.

The tone of the first phrase is kept almost uniform, the *diminuendo* marked being observed. The second phrase (78) starts more softly than the previous one, a slight *crescendo* being made towards bar 80, and then again *diminuendo*.

### Return of the Original Theme

The original melody now returns in its third and most beautiful dress of harmony. Although it is marked *piano*, the melody must sing out intensely, with a *subito* drop in tone at bar 83 which will bring the marvellous change of harmony into even greater relief. Bars 84, 85, 86 are played as before, though perhaps a little more passionately after the wonderful harmony of the preceding bar.

From the *poco crescendo* the pianist can sing out more and more, the left hand being played as warmly as possible. In fact, one must hardly be able to distinguish the harmony from the melody. The sonorities must be throbbing and full throated. This warm *crescendo* should be carried on until the *forte* mark in bar 90. Bars 91 and 92 are the climax of the whole piece. I disagree with the *pianissimo* marked at the end of bar 92, because I feel that it is wrong to let down so suddenly the passionate climax that has been aroused, and therefore I advise that this next phrase be played in exactly the same way as when it occurred earlier as regards *legato* and distribution of tone, but it must sing out in a good round *mezzo-forte* and in a most dignified manner.

Bar 98 is played *piano*, observing the *diminuendos* in the L.H. This *lento*, which is a variation of the earlier one, should be played not quite so intensely as the previous one, though still more tragically and in a more resigned manner. It will be noticed how, towards the end of this phrase, Brahms has changed the value of some of the notes.

A warm, glowing quality should be infused into the tone throughout the piece.

# CHAPTER IX

# *Manuel de Falla*

Still, when the band, placed just beneath the village cross, struck up a lively Jota he capered nimbly, first with one girl, then with another, snapping his fingers like a pair of castagnettes, with his arms held above his shoulders and waving to and fro.—R. B. CUNNINGHAME GRAHAME, *At Navalcan.*

### DANSE DU MEUNIER

The 'Miller's Dance'[1] is a *farruca*—a national dance belonging to the south of Spain, which is generally danced by men only. It is difficult to find words with which to express the intense rhythm, the mixture of pride, grace and even brutality with which Spaniards dance this *farruca*. The student is well advised, therefore, not only to read Alarcón's famous work, *El Corregidor* (which can be found in Martin Armstrong's excellent translation in many public libraries) but everything he can find which treats of Andalusian life and custom, being wary, however, of the enormous mass of romantic and vulgar rubbish which has been written about the Spaniard and the Andaluz in particular.

I have often pointed out how one art is linked up with another, and that it is absolutely necessary for us to know all we can of the painting, literature, dancing, music of every

[1] From *The Three-Cornered Hat.*

country. Just as one cannot have internationality with nationality, I feel it is impossible to understand one art without some knowledge of all arts. The first seed is the same, it is the individual reaction to the fundamental emotion which differentiates the mode of expression.

There is considerable brutality in Spanish and Moorish music and dancing, a brutality which often alternates rapidly with the utmost tenderness, or again, with a languorous sensuality. If I may hazard the opinion, I would say, however, that the temperamental idiom does not lie merely in this alternation, but in the persistence of one mood and one music within the other and in the inner essential unity of alternation. Composers like Debussy and de Falla indicate this nuance in their titles and *tempos*. There is a piece by Debussy called *La Puerta del Viño*, which describes a Spanish scene. The *tempo* is *Mouvement de Habañera*—a *habañera* is another Spanish dance —and Debussy directs it to be played '*avec brusques oppositions d'extrême violence, et de passionnée douceur*'. And again in Falla's exquisite Spanish piece *Andaluza*, he marks it '*très rythmé et avec un sentiment sauvage*'.

Remember that however violent one's feelings may be in interpreting this music it is necessary to have complete control of them. A Spaniard has command of himself and, whatever his emotions, his pride and dignity never desert him.

All these qualities therefore must be conveyed in the interpretation of this little piece.


### Speed and Rhythm

Falla's metronome mark is important—sixty to the minim. It is essential that this piece should not be played too quickly.

I always work at it myself, until the last page, with the metronome. The first chords of the second and fourth bars, just before the *diminuendos*, are the principal accents. All this passage must be played absolutely *dead in time*, with extreme care in the fifth bar to start the drum taps, very softly, for that is what the little group of semiquavers should sound like. One must be careful in bars 2, 4, 6, not to hurry the triplets. All notes in the *ff* chord on G major should be played out equally loudly, with a brilliant and brassy *timbre*. The drum tapping comes back in the next bar.

Now, I have a very bad stretch, and I dare say it will surprise many readers to know that I cannot stretch nine notes in my left hand, and that I can only stretch nine in the right by putting my thumb and finger down one at a time. In bar 8 I have made a slight alteration which will help other pianists with the same disability, and which yet does not make the slightest difference to the actual sound. I leave out the quaver F in the bass in the second half of each crotchet beat.

As there is F in the R.H. the bass F is not missed. Every chord in the bar must be accented. In the next bar it will be seen that the second chord which is marked *pp* should be played all with the R.H. so as to leave the L.H. free for the low E in the next bar. After the low E in this bar 10, the chord is played with the R.H., the L.H. being used again on the quaver group, with the little finger on the E. Care must be taken that all the notes in this *pp* chord sound absolutely together, but the E played with the little finger should sound slightly predominant, the other notes of the chord being played with a very soft *portamento*.

## The Tune

The *portamento* lines which are placed over every other quaver in the L.H. should cause no perplexity. If a slight *portamento* accent can be given there it is all to the good, but I think these marks are really a hint to keep the rhythm rigid. The tune must sing out in a most proud way. Someone watching me play this piece remarked that I unconsciously straightened my back and threw up my head when playing this tune. It must be played with great feeling, but nevertheless proudly and triumphantly. I make a gentle, but sudden, *diminuendo*, at the first half of bar 14, playing very languorously. This gives one a chance to make a little *crescendo* in the next bar, making a lot of the second quaver F. Bars 16 and 17 I make a *rubato* thus:

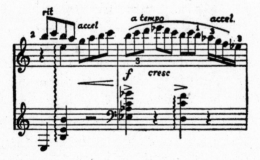

Falla actually writes out a *rubato* in this way in his *Nights in the Gardens of Spain*. It does not matter if the tone is hard: it will be remembered that Debussy's instructions are to use brusque changes in tone. The slurs over bars 16 and 17 are to be regarded as phrase marks, not as *legato* marks, because the passage must be played non-*legato*. This passage should be practised with hand rotation, using the hand as well as the fingers in whatever direction they are moving. The arm should be kept light and all exertion should cease directly the sound in key descent is reached. This, and a non-*legato*, will help to achieve the ringing brilliant tone that is required for this passage.

### The Next Phrase

Bar 18 is played exactly as at the beginning, and in bar 19 it will be easier to take the lower B♮ of the R.H. with the L.H., thus:

The pedal is changed once in a bar from bar 21. In this bar the melody is in the R.H. and the L.H. triplets should be just gently woven into the theme. In the orchestral version of this piece there is a *glissando* on the harp in place of the L.H. accompaniment. I have already given directions about playing two against three. No attempt should be made to fit the two parts one into the other, but each hand should be practised separately, getting the rhythms fixed in the mind. When they are played together, these two rhythms should go on independently of one another. The beat itself is the important thing and not its divisions and, by thinking from each beat to the next beat, one will find oneself fitting the two very slightly different parts quite naturally in their time places.

### Fingering and Stretches

Here again it does not matter if the tone is a little hard. In bar 29 I prefer a *mezzo-piano* to the *mezzo-forte* marked, the next bars being played without haste: the triplets in bar 31 make an *accelerando*. A tight hold should be kept on the rhythm, with a tiny accent on every crotchet beat, the effect being achieved by a huge *crescendo*.

Those pianists who cannot stretch a tenth may spread the three L.H. chords in bar 32, accenting the top note and this fingering will help with the next bar:

It will also enable the inside notes to be played more lightly and the thumb will be able to jump about more easily. Each crotchet beat and note, every note, must be accented. The first accented note in bar 35 must be played as loudly as possible and crisply and rhythmically. It will be easier to take the L.H. A with the R.H. thumb, the thumb playing both the B and A.

In bar 36, as much as possible must be made of the *subito pp* by playing very softly, but intensely rhythmically, and getting a short *tapping* kind of tone. I am using the word 'tapping' as though one's fingers were drumsticks, and as if they were playing on the vellum surface of a drum. Again I must emphasize what I said about not playing the triplets too quickly.

### An Elaboration of the Tune

From bars 44 to 52 we have an elaboration of the tune we had earlier and here the imitation of a harp *glissando* is more exact. The L.H. must be played very softly and should be as even as a string of pearls. The B and A in the R.H. in bars 44, 46, 47 and so on, are played both with the thumb. In bar 47, the melody is in the right hand and should be sung out very languorously. Care must be taken to keep the L.H. which crosses over the right, very soft—it is just an echo of the L.H. part in bar 45. The B in bass in bars 45 and 49 is important. In the orchestra the 'celli and double basses probably have this note *pizzicato* in addition to the harp. In bar 51, the L.H. is again an echo, but must still be expressive. It will be noticed that in bar 52 there is a slight change in the R.H.

*The Last Section*

From here to the end is one long *crescendo* and *accelerando*. The pedal is changed once in a bar and for each quaver in the L.H. (treble clef) the L.H. should cross over the R.H.

This section begins very softly and very slowly and, however softly it is played, a little pointed accent on the L.H. treble quaver should be given. By now it is clear that I play as spontaneously as possible—in fact as if I were creating for the first time the piece of music as I play it. Nevertheless, the intellect must be the basis of all interpretation: it cannot be left to the emotion of the moment. This *crescendo* and *accelerando* must therefore be planned out beforehand, or the student will find that he gets loud too soon or ends up so quickly that there is no time to get in any notes at all.

I lay out this last section (from bar 53) superficially very much as Falla has indicated. The first four bars are played very softly, without getting louder or quicker and the next four bars get gradually louder. At bar 61, and for the next four bars, the tone which is arrived at should be maintained, merely getting quicker. By bar 65 a pretty quick pace will have been achieved and one should go on getting louder until by bar 69 *ff* will have been reached. If it is not possible to stretch the R.H. chords it will not matter very much if the lower D in the R.H. and the lower B in the next bar are omitted, the R.H. passage being carried on as in bars 53 to 68, only an octave higher.

Although the pace is getting quicker and quicker, the rhythm must be kept absolutely rigid to the end and in bar 75 the lower E in the second chord may be omitted if it presents a difficulty.

# CHAPTER X

## *Debussy*

'CLAIR DE LUNE'

Rendez-moi, o, rendez-moi mon ciel et ma musique.
LOUIS ARAGON.

Many artists whom I have heard on the concert platform seem to whisper to me, sitting in the audience: 'I really don't know what to do with this piece.'

This is perhaps specially true of Debussy's 'Clair de Lune', seemingly so simple, that is, with no great technical difficulties, easy to memorize, rather quiet, and not very quick. We all know this piece; we all love it, it is a great favourite with amateurs: but its apparent simplicity is a delusion and a snare, and because it is so easily and quickly learned, its inner message may never reveal itself. Therefore, I am not surprised when pupils, presenting this piece for a lesson, boastfully declare they have not found it necessary to give much time to it: however, before they are halfway through, it is soon clear they are, like the artists I have described above, sitting in a vacuum, hoping it will 'come off' and that the music will give them the clue to the interpretation and performance.

142

In most of Debussy's piano pieces, and certainly in this one in particular, colour and rhythm are interdependent.

In all music, and especially in the slow movements, there must be absolute perfection of rhythm and line, and within this framework the inner time values must be accurate; additional accents are not necessary if the absolute value of notes is observed. This involves 'going all the way' with the composer; not a fraction of the phrases or sounds must be shortened or lengthened. Moreover, one must think not only of WHAT one is doing at that moment, but one must listen for the sounds ahead so that they take their right place in the general structure. Thus, if the absolute value of notes is observed, extra accenting is not necessary, nor is the hurrying of a subsidiary phrase. For instance, the quavers after the long notes at the beginning of 'Clair de Lune' are often treated as arabesques, whereas they are really a continuation of the melody, therefore demanding strict durations which should be phrased *towards* the next long note. The student rightly feels that if the quavers stand out the phrase will be lopsided, so he hurries them; but if these shorter notes were played with a diminished tone, there would be no need to hurry them because they would no longer stand out. Therefore, it will be seen that colour and rhythm are inextricably mixed and the exaggeration of one distorts the other. The very harmonies are a guide to the line and colour. This is true not only of Debussy, but of all music, especially the dramatic. If the student is in any doubt as to how to "paint in" his colours, he should let the harmony tell him. The secret of when to increase the volume or to drop tone suddenly, to diminish with one hand and to increase with the other, is in the harmony of the piece itself.

The etherial, poignant and often mysterious quality of Debussy's piano pieces, demand a performance in which there are many vibrations to each sound. My own secret of getting this nebulous tone is to start the movement of the key from below the surface level. It is as if one had an imaginary keyboard surface one-fifth lower than it actually is. We must rest enough weight on the key to depress it one-fifth, before we begin the movement towards the sound point. This is extremely difficult and takes a great deal of practice. If, however, the student cannot master this, he should move the key rather slowly all the way, otherwise the quality of the tone will be too piercing. One uses this movement for Chopin (see p. 113) but naturally one increases the speed of the movement on its journey, from the *top* of the key and not from below the surface in order to get the piercing quality of tone required for his more poignant and singing music. As can be observed from this lesson, I consider natural gifts are very often a hindrance and prevent the student from penetrating to the very heart and meaning of the music.

## Lesson on Debussy

As I have said above, keep the quavers in the first lines strictly in time because they are the continuation of the melody. They must be phrased towards the long notes. The quavers should be played more softly than the dotted crotchets and the dotted crotchets more softly than the dotted minims. In that way there will be balance between the Durations, and the line and structure will, therefore, be equally poised.

In bars 5 and 6 there should be a slight *crescendo*; on bar 7 this nuance of tone should diminish again. The student will notice, especially on this first page of 'Clair de Lune', quavers in groups of two sometimes take the place of groups of three quavers. This occurs at bars 1 to 3, 13 to 14, and also later in the piece. Very great care must be taken that the twos, being slower, are equal in spacing, because there is a temptation when one plays two in a group, after three, to hurry the two. If we think it thus, it will be in time:

Bar 15. It is advisable that the first of every beat should be a little weightier in attack—this is an infinitely small nuance—than the succeeding quavers. Also one must not get on to the second note in the group of threes too soon.

From bar 19, keep the rising bass in mind; automatically making a *crescendo* is no use unless you think the musical reason for this increase, and musically it is the mounting basses here that build the phrase up and provide the need for getting more tone and animation.

Now you will, of course, have to leave the sound of these dotted minims in the lower bass to be carried on by the pedal because your left hand is needed higher up. Although you let go with the fingers and sustain only with the pedal, the minims must continue in your mind as sounds progressing on to the next minim.

When spreading chords, remember that the first bass note is of extreme importance and the pedal should be changed, not when you get to the top of the chord, but from the first note. This, of course, applies to spread chords in any part of the piece.

From *un poco mosso*, the student must try and find three different levels of tone; this is very difficult, and these three levels must continue quite apart from the nuances which will be introduced, according to the harmonies. The semiquavers must be very quiet, but the lowest note in the bass should sound out because the harmony is built on it and the melody in the R.H. must sound out still more than the bass note: all this, mark you, within the limit of the *pianissimo* indicated by the composer.

Change of *tempo* should be very slight; just enough to indicate that it is not 'pedestrian'.

Care must be taken in the *crescendo*, bar 29; this should only be very small, as the next level of bars is only *piano*.

The student must remember that there is a long way towards the *forte* on the next page, so he should keep his *crescendo* well back. In bars 37 to 39 he must be very careful not to get too shrill a tone in the R.H. (melody). Nor must he push the time too much forward from *en animant* as the *crescendo* will give the impression of gathered momentum.

In bar 40 (third page) drop the tone on the third beat almost like a *subito*, but don't let this nuance stop the flow of the piece.

When returning to the *tempo primo* (*ppp*) the student must remember to keep the semiquavers very even and not to play them in a melodic way as he would more in a Haydn Sonata. They should be considered as just harmony. Where there is, in the melody, the last note in the bar tied on to the next he must be very careful to give that first (tied) note its absolute full time in Duration and not come too soon on to the ensuing group of notes.

I would advise the student, for the first four bars of *Tempo*

*Primo* to use only one change of pedal for every bar: if he feels he must change it, only use 'half-pedal'. Later he will have to change the pedal on the third beat of each bar as well as on the first, as the harmonies alter. He must be very careful of the harmonic progression in the L.H. in the last two bars of this period, A♭ in the L.H. (dotted minim), going to the G♭ (dotted crotchet) bottom of spread chord.

In the second bar of the *morendo*, just before the end, he should use what I call the 'French tone' for the dotted crotchet in the R.H., that is, slightly metallic, but well rounded in quality all the same, like the *timbre* of the French language. If he pronounces the word '*timbre*' in the right way, slightly nasally, he will understand what I mean.

# CHAPTER XI

# *R. Vaughan Williams*

O, my love, how comely now,
And how beautiful art thou,
Thou of dove-like eyes a paire,
Shining hast within thy haire,
And thy locks like kidlings bé,
Which from Gilead Hill we see.

(SONG 13)

HYMN-TUNE PRELUDE
(*Dedicated to Harriet Cohen*)

As I have said in another chapter, the function of the great composer is to take up and transform into his own personal idiom (or mode of musical speech) what has been communally experienced. This idiom must be a common possession, but broad enough to allow a personal vocabulary to the composer. The basis of Vaughan Williams's idiom, which owes much to his love and understanding of our great heritage of Tudor and folk music, provides him with a universal musical language which he uses in a characteristic personal way, and drawing inspiration from this music of the soil, his own has the very essence of things in it.

John Donne, aware of this essence, wrote of God in one of his great sermons thus: 'An angel in an angel, a stone in a

148

stone, a straw in a straw.' Similarly one can describe Vaughan
Williams's music as a 'tune in a tune'. Perhaps this is most
strongly evident in works where he has gone to the Old
Testament for inspiration. In particular I would choose his
settings for the Book of Job and the wonderful evocation of
The Song of Songs in Flos Campi. The metrical version of
one of the Songs, called in the English Hymnal, Song 13,
has been set to music by the Elizabethan composer Orlando
Gibbons, and it is this lovely tune that Vaughan Williams
has used for the chorale-like theme round which he has
woven the serene and beautiful music which he calls Hymn-
Tune Prelude on Song 13.

Among his very few piano pieces I naturally have a great affection for his Piano Concerto which he wrote for me. This is a work which I feel opened up the way to his 4th and 5th Symphonies, and I can recognize much of the emotional and technical 'climates' of these symphonies from my own necessarily long and devotional study of the Concerto. But for this small collection of lessons, I have chosen the Hymn-Tune Prelude as being more fitting for the scope of this little book.

The great difficulty about this piece is the part playing and the student will have gently to hold notes down for quite a long time. He will also sometimes have to use the same finger or thumb on succeeding notes, so he should get used to sliding silently from one note to another. Where bars occur with really difficult fingering, I will give examples.

Having a very small hand, where there are great jumps in the L.H., such as tenths, I have taken the top note with the R.H. This is practicable in most places.

I always feel that it is in slow music that the pianist shows whether or not he is an artist, and faults in rhythm (fundamental rhythm, not just *tempo*) have a way of standing out in a glaring, conspicuous manner.

The introductary eight bars are rather ardent, and quite different in quality from Orlando Gibbons's chorale-like theme which starts on page 2.

Even this theme should not be sung with such bell-like tones as in a Bach Chorale, because the verse from the Song of Songs is, after all, a love poem.

Do not retard the *tempo* in the bar before the Canto (last bar, page 1) and in that bar, make a *diminuendo*, including any nuances of tone within that *diminuendo*; in fact, start it from the last beat of the previous bar, thus:

150

Page 2 is very much more difficult to play contrapuntally, as the long notes of the tune have to be held on for different lengths of time from the long notes in the counterpoint. This can be extremely muddling. Sometimes, to make matters easier, I take over a note of the tune to the L.H. For instance, the B to the word 'Oh' (1st bar, page 2) I play with the L.H. and resume the R.H. thumb on C at the end of the bar.

In the next bar, the notes A and G which are set to 'come-ly' I play with the L.H., using the thumb for both notes, continuing this on to the next bar. Again, on the last line of that page for the B on the word 'Thou' I use the L.H. and do not resume the R.H. until the next bar on D, set to the word 'dove'.

Great care must be taken in pedalling bar 2, page 3. The canto is in the R.H., the thumb sliding from one note to the other. As this is a very contrapuntal bar, care must be taken that the D is held down with the thumb whilst the pedal changes on the third beat, and after that we must trust to the pedal to hold the D on because we shall need the thumb temporarily elsewhere (E on the counterpoint) and the thumb comes back to the canto on the C and B ('ing').

A very important nuance I use myself is on the fourth bar,

page 3. For the word 'haire' make a *subito pianissimo*, even so the G of the melody must stand out a little. This can be most moving if rightly judged.

In the last line of page 3, bar 1, I use the R.H. thumb for the melody and the fingering for the quavers must be very carefully done to get even *legato* playing. I finger it thus:

After the chorale is finished on the word 'see', keep the tone up so that the original composition of Vaughan Williams here to the end, as on page 1, is shown to be, as it is, a lovely continuation in mood and feeling of the original Hymn Tune. Take the whole page in which to quieten, ending up the piece as marked, *pp*.

In the first page, care must be taken over this appealing little phrase:

A    B    A

which comes as a refrain again and again, appearing for the last time in the L.H. in the last bar at the end of the page. This must be played wistfully, and however varying the tone (when it comes again in the last page there is a general *diminuendo*) it should stand out and be played with the dynamics indicated by the composer.

# CHAPTER XII

# *Bartok*

Because I know that time is always time
And place is always and only place
And what is actual is actual only for one time
And only for one place . . .

T. S. ELIOT.

Many of the major works of Bartok are comparatively small-scaled, the musical thought finding as it were another dimension. This extension gives them a strength and a quality of permanence that is not always found in some of his larger works where the symbolic content[1] makes them somewhat remote and withdrawn. The intensity of this taut and concentrated musical thinking is, to my mind, of greater value than all the grandiose outpourings of a Liszt or a Bruckner.

Bartok had an innate feeling for complicated and subtle rhythms, and like Stravinsky in his earlier works must have drawn them from some ancient folk tribal memory. It may be that these atavistic promptings caused him to use so freely tunes and rhythms gleaned from the land and shared with the peasants.

His independence, his iconoclasm, his technical device and

[1] See *Musical Companion*, p. 3, Chapter 7, by Edward Dent.

dexterity, as in the piano concertos, might blind the superficial student of modern music to the great depth and sustained power of works such as the string quartets, which are among the greatest music ever achieved.

The great French masters Milhaud and Honeggar in the tense and haunting beauty of their later works approach nearest to the strange territory that Bartok inhabits, and breathe with him the atmosphere of that rare clime, though there is a more obvious sensuous bloom in their music than in the austerer lines of the Hungarian Master. Kodaly, his illustrious compatriot, would seem to demand wider and more airy spaces for his creative adventuring.

## MIKROKOSMOS

### SIX DANCES IN BULGARIAN RHYTHM

Dedicated

to

#### MISS HARRIET COHEN

From the beginning of my pianistic career new works by Schönberg, Bax, 'Les Six', (Honegger, Milhaud, Auric, etc.), Kodaly, Pizzetti, Hindemith, Malipiero, Turina, Vaughan Williams, Sibelius, Janáček, Villa-Lobos, De Falla, Shostakovitch, etc., were confided into my hands for first performances; no dedication gave me such profound happiness and sense of fulfilment in my career than the surprise presentation by him in New York of Bartok's superlative piece for piano, a whole world of music in twenty-one pages—the Bulgarian Dances, the last, most difficult, and summit of his great opus for the piano, the Mikrokosmos, which he dedicated to me.

It is very difficult indeed to achieve the exact metronome timing of the composer. I think that in a performance I have taken a few seconds longer in the First Dance and it is a very great temptation to finish up the Third Dance twenty seconds too early, but I am sure the composer would not have minded these very slight variations within say twenty or twenty-five seconds.

*No.* 1 $\left(\dfrac{4\ 2\ 3}{8}\right)$

·If the left-hand quaver passages are not played too loudly from bar 4 onwards, the right-hand syncopated tune can sound out very clearly, but not with a forced *forte* otherwise by the time we get to *più forte* in the third bar on page 36 the hammer can penetrate through the string. If possible, change the finger on the repeated notes (R.H.) in case the action of the piano is not very sensitive and quick. In bar 3, page 36, I use the fourth finger on the second quaver in the L. H. thus:

In this first part the essential rhythms of 1 2 3 4, 1 2, 1 2 3 must be kept absolutely strict.

In the top line of page 37 because of the occasional breaking up of the first four quavers it is easier to keep the rhythm in mind by mentally accenting the second group (1, 2) that is the third crotchet. At the *meno vivo* the *crescendo* should be played as marked but, commencing immediately, it should be on a very small scale indeed, only reaching about *mezzo-piano* in the third bar. This level of tone should be kept for a few beats while the *accelerando* gets under way and then the *crescendo* should be taken up again at the end of the fourth bar, reaching *mezzo-forte* on the fifth bar with a final *crescendo* up to the *forte*. The fingering is difficult in the third bar of this second part: it is wiser in these difficult passages to use Liszt's device of going from the fifth finger to the fourth instead of turning under the thumb, so:

I do not quite take up *tempo I* as marked in the last line of page 37 as I think having only one bar for the *poco allargando* on the next page would lead too suddenly to the *calmo*, therefore I use a 'quasi' *tempo I*. I expect it is this deliberate hold back which has caused me to be a few seconds over time in my rendering of this piece, but I think the composer would have agreed.

In the fifth bar before the end the fundamental rhythm of 4 2 3 will be thrown into relief if an accent is given on the fifth quaver, that is the first of the '2' group in the right hand. This will hold the bar together and will enable the student to give an accent on the third octave in the left hand (coming immediately before the right-hand accent) which will have the effect of extreme syncopation. The last two quavers (octaves) in the third bar from the end I share between both hands.

*No. 2* $\left(\dfrac{2\ 2\ 3}{8}\right)$

The three bar-from-bar phrases should be separated into very monotonous buzzing sort of rhythms and shortened staccato measures; care must be taken to alternate the series of *mezzo-fortes* with the *fortes* as shown in the composer's markings. In bar 4, which is the beginning of the *forte* section, care must be taken to keep the 12 12 very short and crisp and the 1 2 3 *legato*. This goes on for a set period of four bars. Apart from the initial *sforzando* in the next three bars, as in the first three bars, the tone must be kept to a straight *mezzo-forte*; the next *forte* section is only two bars instead of the previous three. In the strange scale passage in quavers at the end of the page take care to keep the two bars at a level and quieter tone as marked. These alternating *fortes* and *mezzo-fortes* should be played with the abrupt change-over that is the composer's intention, but at the last bar on page 39 great care should be taken in starting the *mezzo-forte* as there is a long way to go before the *martellato*. Tremendous verve and gusto must be put into the ensuing bars and the speed should be kept up unflaggingly. The buzzing, monotonous tone about which I have spoken above can be induced largely by skilful use of the pedal and with the *diminuendo* the tone should be kept at a level and rather dull colour from the *mezzo-piano*.

Care must be taken in the last four bars to keep strictly to the initial dance rhythms, even though this may not be apparent to the hearer because of the many rests. Except for the *ritenuto* in the eleventh bar before the end, the *tempo* must be absolutely strict and should approximate as nearly as possible to the composer's metronome markings.

*No. 3* $\dfrac{(5)}{8}$

The little introduction of four bars should be played in a very light manner and can be taken at a shade faster rate than the actual 'tune' which is very like a Scottish one with the 'snap' in its third bar. These very slight alternations of *tempo*, between the striking rhythmical tune and the delicate interlude, should be kept up to the end of the piece but must be almost imperceptible. As in the previous dance, the composer keeps the several sections at different levels of tone, thus, *p. leggero* alternates with *f, marc.*

If at the bottom of page 42, the student finds it difficult to hold the thumb on the G for several bars, he should put the pedal down halfway through the fourth bar, keeping it right on to the sixth; this would enable him to let go the thumb and he can then show the descending accents in each phrase on G, F and E.

The *p. leggero* should be a very quiet murmuring in the right hand. The *crescendo molto* at the bottom of page 43 leads to one of the most remarkable phrases in the set of dances; it is a canon on a variation of the original theme of this piece; note the slight change in the last bar of the page where the syncopated lilt comes at the *beginning* of each statement of the canon. The parts and indeed the hands should be practised slowly and separately, and then should be played up to time with the metronome. Although it is extremely hard to play up to time, it is easier as regards complicated rhythms once they have been mastered slowly.

All the last part should be played most delicately, taking care in the last bars that the tone is diminished to a real *pianissimo*.

## No. 4 $\left(3 \frac{2}{8} 3\right)$

This dance should be taken not only as an exercise in dance rhythm, but as a very charming and bright tune. Care must be taken that the second group of two quavers are not drawn out and do not sound like a badly played three. For practising it is well to accent the first note of the last group of three and this prevents one from staying too long on the second group. Of course this accent must not be shown in performance, the most important accent naturally coming on the first of the bar.

I like the tune in the left hand to be played in a very tempestuous manner.

Note how the original theme changes in the last line at the beginning of the second bar.

This happens again in the first part of the next page; the tune states crotchet then quaver instead of the quaver crotchet of the earlier theme. The change of rhythm is transferred to the last beat when the tune starts *piano* at the end of the first line, page 46, and instead of being crotchet quaver is quaver crotchet. This, added to the quaver accompaniment in the left hand makes it all extremely difficult and complicated. In the *forte* passage the tune returns in the left hand to its original layout but it is made more difficult by the quaver rest in the right hand at the end of the little trumpet-like chords. Here again the hands should be practised separately, and certainly for practise, even for performance, a good accent should be given on the third beat of the right hand, the tune in the left hand being accented on the first beat. The last line is even harder because there are more rests in the right hand.

For the second line of page 47 the composer's fingering in

the right hand is excellent; I think it would be a good plan to put on the soft pedal for this whole phrase. In the *ritenuto* bar before the *meno mosso* the rhythm should be kept steady in the left hand. In the *meno mosso* it will be observed that the left hand is really playing the same passage in all four bars although they start each time one chord higher, therefore care must be taken to get the same fingering. From the second bar onwards, I personally use the fifth finger at the bottom of each chord in the left hand for the first half of the bar, and for the last three chords I use 4 5 4, thus:

I think *tempo I* should be not quite up to time, thus making the *allargando* not so sudden. At the top of page 48 the composer's fingering (L.H.) is excellent and the student would be well advised to keep to it. Here the *tempo* should be strictly up to time and the alternation of *piano* with *forte* very marked. No change of colour in the last line.

## No. 5 $\left(\dfrac{2\ 2\ 2\ 3}{8}\right)$

This dance should be very lightly handled and at the beginning anyway, practically unaccented. The alternations of *staccato* and the two *legato* notes at the end of the bar will provide enough variety. At bar 5 the hands are apt to get tangled with one another and for those few bars I keep the left hand above the right (*sopra*). The last line, page 49, is not so hard to play if strict attention is paid to the 1 2 3 at the end of the bar, and the student can then think the previous groups 1 2, 1 2 3 4 or 1 2, 1 2, 1 2, or 1 2 3 4, 1 2; concentrating the accent on the end group of 1 2 3 holds these six difficult bars together. For bar 3 the right hand should be above the left hand in case of tangling. The very end should be worked up to a great *forte*, dying away as marked, and should be played with a subtle and nervous energy. All the last page should be very crisp and short and not over-accented; as in the beginning the effect is made with dynamics.

## No. 6 (3 3 2)
### —
### 6

No. 6 is the finest technical study of all the dances. The broken octaves are very difficult to play especially for a small hand and need a flexible but nevertheless strong turn of the wrist. Among pianists there are arguments as to whether on the top half the thumb should be played twice or whether it should be changed on the repeated note to the second finger. This indeed is a very vexed question and I notice the composer is not getting involved as he has not marked any fingering.

The beginning of page 52 is a very good exercise for repeated notes in the R. H. The composer again uses his device of canon at the *forte*.

I do not think the student will find this last dance very difficult from a rhythmical point of view, but technically it is the hardest and to be played up to time requires a tremendous amount of work. The *tempo* should be steady up to *double forte marcatissimo* and then the chords can move on, giving a sense of urgency rather than that of increased speed.

In the repeated notes in the middle of page 54 it is as well to follow the composer's fingering, and at the top of page 55 use the same fingers as in the corresponding passage at the top of page 52.

Should the student desire to play some of the dances separately if he thinks that his audience would not be able to take in all six, I advise him to take three and play them in this order: No. 2, No. 3, No. 5.

# CHAPTER XIII

## *Arnold Bax*

ὥς τέ με κουράων ἀμφήλυθε θῆλυς ἀυτή·
νυμφάων, αἵ ἔχουσ᾽ ὀρέων αἰπεινὰ κάρηνα
καί πηγὰς ποταμῶν καί πίσεα ποιήεντα.
                                            HOMER, *Odyssey*.

### 'NEREID'

In a previous chapter I said that all the parts of the Bach
Choral should move to their appointed places. Similarly the
more you study the music of Arnold Bax the more you will
find that his contrapuntal parts likewise move logically. It is
this quality, I think, which marks him as a direct musical
descendant of William Byrd, the greatest English composer
of the sixteenth century.

Bax has often told me that he considers his music to be
directly derived from nature. When he wrote this piece,
*Nereid*, he had vaguely in mind some sort of water nymph of
Greek mythological times.

### The Lilting Figures

The R.H. melody must be made to sound as clear and cool
as water itself, and this will be done by taking care to play
the semiquavers at the end of the second and the fourth beats

much more softly than the long notes which precede and follow them. The reason for this is that the music demands that its time be thought of as two in a bar, i.e. two dotted minims instead of four dotted crotchets. This gives the lilt that is obviously wanted on to the first and third beats, the second and fourth beats being tied. It should also be noted that in the fourth bar, at the end of the second beat, there are three semiquavers instead of the two in the preceding bar, which very slightly delays the little lilting phrase. Another composer, less fastidious and careful, would have written the two notes A♯ and E♯, as before, and marked a *rubato* above them, Bax, however, preferred to write out his *rubato*. The same thing occurs at the end of the fifth bar.

In the second beat of the sixth bar, the pianist will be playing four semiquavers in the time of six and he should remember to play these four slowly enough to avoid reaching the next beat too soon. The melody must be allowed to sing out clearly while the accompaniment must always be played very softly. In the last half of the eighth bar I make a *diminuendo*, singing clearly again on the first note of the ninth bar. At the end of the tenth bar it will be seen that the little lilt has an extra note, nevertheless it must be played in strict time. This is the fourth way of writing the lilting figure which the composer has used. Here are all four ways:

*Second Section*

This fourth variation of the lilt is now continued, alternating with the third for several bars. Concentration upon the principal beats will make the rhythmic playing of these semiquaver passages quite easy. Here again is music whose rhythm must be listened to attentively by the player.

Although this part is more expressive, it must be kept very cool in feeling. It is interesting to notice, for instance, how the second part of the bar becomes, in the L.H., four semiquavers played in the time of six, thus making the second part of the bar more languid than the first.

The sixteenth bar is marked *forte*, but this mark is only relative, and it must be realized that the whole piece is played within a very small dynamic scale. After the *forte*, an immediate *diminuendo* in the L.H. of bar 16 is necessary, and from this bar until bar 19, care is also needed in playing the first note in the bass clearly, thus indicating the direction of the harmonic modulation. For several bars from this point there is an alternation of A major and A minor. Contrary to the marking of the copy, I think it best to play the last half of bar 20 suddenly (*subito*) very softly, as if the nymph had disappeared into the water, the tone suddenly coming out again singing clearly as before.

*Bars 19 to 27*

From the nineteenth bar, the L.H. should become very quiet now that the new and, for the time being, almost stationary harmony has been reached. In the twenty-second bar the player must move straight on without lingering over the quaver passage in the R.H. In fact, for the next three or four bars, right up to the new key signature, the music should be kept in steady movement.

### Bars 27 to 31. *The Test Section*

The student's playing of the passage beginning with the new key signature will show whether he had really absorbed what I have written in my lesson on the Chopin Etude, concerning the playing of one rhythm in one hand against a different rhythm in the other. So important is it that again I must warn the student against trying to fit the two parts one into the other. Each hand should be practised separately, so that the rhythms are mentally appropriated. During performance it is important to listen to these two rhythms going on independently of one another.

The whole of this present passage should be studied, each hand separately. The fact that there are two quavers to a beat in one hand and three quavers to a beat in the other hand should not cause perplexity. All that concerns the pianist is the beat itself: not its divisions. If the student thinks from each beat to the next he will find himself fitting the two very slightly different parts quite naturally in their time places. At the end of the second beat in bar 27 the little lilt in the R.H. comes immediately after the D♯ in the L.H. At the end of the fourth beat the L.H. plays the same *tempo* as the R.H., so that in this case there will be no trouble at all. At the end of the second beat in the next bar, Bax has again written out his *rubato*, and instead of the R.H. lilt coming immediately after the L.H., as in the previous bar, it will arrive just a shade later. In the same bar four semiquavers in the R.H. against six in the L.H. again present themselves, and these should not be fitted against one another, but just played so that one is conscious of moving surely to the next beat. In any other way it is hopeless to expect to secure rhythmic precision.

In bar 29 the semiquaver D in the R.H. is a misprint for B. I find the semiquaver passage in the L.H. in bar 30 is best fingered so: 2 5 1 4 2 1. The pedal should be changed twice in a bar in this section and always with every change in the harmony. This will mean, in general, that the pedal must be changed twice in a bar throughout the piece.

The feeling of water which is present throughout this piece has come more into the foreground in this section. Now we have quite a cascade, and in keeping with this a clear laughing quality must be given to the playing.

## The Climax

The thirty-first bar should be played very softly, making a *crescendo* from the first beat (minim beat) to the next beat, and again to the first beat of the next bar, making *waves* of sound. From bar 31 both hands are playing four dotted crotchets to the bar. In bar 33, the L.H. has a singing passage which becomes more prominent, although the idea of waves should always be present in the R.H., the climax being built up until bar 34. A good fingering for the L.H. semiquaver passage in bar 34 is: 2 5 1 4 2 1 3, both notes of the octave C being taken with the R.H. The *ritenuto* in bar 36 should be very small. From bar 37 both hands play the original *tempo* of four dotted crotchets to the bar.

The L.H. must be carried over the R.H. for the chord of

the third beat of bar 41, and the second chord in the last bar played thus: the first four notes with the L.H., the next four, i.e. beginning with the B, with the R.H., the top D♯ being taken with the L.H.

And now, from bar 37 onwards, the piece should be played in a most tranquil manner, even more coolly than at the beginning, without the slightest trace of hurrying the little lilting figure. Another error to be guarded against is that of landing on the crotchet beats with percussion violence, for this would destroy all that sense of grace and tranquillity which now pervades the music. The crotchets must be regarded as signposts, towards which one moves with all the delicacy one can secure, giving to every beat all the time that is allotted to it.

# INDEX

# INDEX